JUSTIN RHEDRICK

From Bars to Bitcoin

BITCOIN**VEGAN**

First published by BitcoinVegan Transformational Services 2021

Some names and details referenced in this book have been changed to protect the privacy of the individuals mentioned.

First edition

ISBN: 978-1-7378266-0-6

Editing by Erica S. Hernandez
Cover art by Antonio Anderson IG: @coinsaucenews

This book was professionally typeset on Reedsy.
Find out more at reedsy.com

*This book is dedicated to the following people who
had a profound impact on my life.*

*Travis Moore - July 20, 1987-February 18, 2007
Kobe Bryant - August 23, 1978-January 26, 2020
Dairyon Stevenson- May 12, 1989-June 22, 2020
Silas Ross - April 28, 1987-August 11, 2020
Courtney Rhedrick Gant - June 25, 1987-September 21, 2020*

Preface

Thank you for purchasing *From Bars to Bitcoin*. This book will give you great insight into the journey I took from being in prison, to entrepreneurship to all the growth that took place in my life that ultimately led me to Bitcoin. Throughout this book, I tell my story and describe the lessons learned using one of nature's fiercest predators as an example. After studying the tactics and predator mentality of the orca whale, I chose to use this animal as a metaphor for my personal journey. As you move further through this book, I will reveal different aspects of the orca mentality that got me to where I am today. I call these bits of wisdom Orca Moments and hope that you find them useful in your own personal development. Now, here's a little bit of background on why I chose the orca to tell my story.

Illustration by Antonio Anderson

Why the Orca?

I know what you're thinking. Justin, why the hell would I want to be Free Willy and not the great white shark in the movie Jaws? Yeah, trust me I get it. That's why I'm taking this time now to share this with you before you dive into this book (yes, I used the word dive).

The Shark

Now, if you're a parent, and I just made you think of the hit YouTube song "Baby Shark," I truly apologize. And if you're not a parent, you're in for a great ride. Let's take a deep look at a shark. Sharks are said to be the kings of the ocean. They're the most well-known ocean predators, with over a thousand vicious sharp teeth that get replaced each time an older tooth is damaged. The shark is a mindless killing machine that incites fear in everything it encounters. If you ever watch Shark Week on the Discovery Channel, you'll learn a shark has little to no strategy as a solo hunter. Later on, we will see the cons of working alone and the pros of working together as a group. Needless to say, the shark is a real alpha. However, being an alpha has its flaws.

The Orca

Now let's take a look at the orca. Give yourself some time to think of all the things you know about the orca. Chances are, it's not much unless you're into animals or are a marine biologist. Most people's first thought of an orca whale might be the legendary Shamu at SeaWorld or maybe even Free Willy jumping over a wall of rocks to find his freedom.

Don't feel bad because I was once like you. When I was in third grade, I remember loving Free Willy so much I tried to jump over a jacuzzi attached to a pool. That didn't turn out so well. My leg got caught inside the jacuzzi wall, and this day if I hit my leg the wrong way, I can still feel some pain. The crazy thing is I never went to the hospital. My mom patched me up and

I went to school the very next day, almost dragging my leg to walk.

One day I looked up how orcas got the name "killer whales." I headed to YouTube to find the answer, and in one video heard the narrator refer to the orca as the "apex predator of the sea." Now, when you hear something like this your ears perk up a bit and you have to figure out how that's possible. Again, all you mainly hear about are sharks. The first thing I did was find the definition of apex predator. According to the Merriam-Webster dictionary, it's "a predator at the top of a food chain that is not preyed upon by any other animal."

Outside of humans, the orca is at the top of the ocean food chain. Learning this blew my mind. By now you are probably thinking, Justin, what the hell does this have to do with life, business, and furthermore what the hell does this have to do with me? Just relax, I promise it's going to all make sense.

After learning this, I really started thinking a bit deeper. Why wasn't this talked about on TV? Why is the shark glorified as the king of the sea? Why is the shark so popular? I did some more searching on YouTube and found a video called "Why Killer Whales Are APEX Predators!" What I learned astounded me.

What makes the orca the apex predator?

The name orca comes from the mythical Orcus, the Roman god of death. Their reputation as the "killer whale" likely stems from sailors who long ago may have seen orcas preying on whale species. The sailors called orcas "whale killers" but over time the name morphed into "killer whale." Ironically, orcas are not whales, but belong to the dolphin family. They are known to hunt prey of any size including great white sharks and, yes, even whales.

Senses

Orcas have acute underwater hearing. They can hear each other from 10 miles away. They use noise to hunt and detect the size of their prey. This is why they don't attack humans.

Hunting Strategy

Orcas are highly sophisticated and creative hunters. They work in a pod using all types of strategies and techniques to take down prey. Ingenuity and hunting intelligence is passed down from one generation to the next.

Orcas adapt their strategy according to their prey. They locate their target using echolocation, a method of interpreting underwater soundwaves. Once their target is found, there's no hope for the prey. When hunting for fish, orcas will surround the school, blow bubbles at them or hit them with their tail to stun them. They then pick off the shocked fish.

Orcas will change their hunting method for fast-swimming fish like tuna. Instead of trying to catch tuna, orca will just chase them with the goal of tiring out the fish. After their prey is exhausted, they eat them. They are also known to do something called wave washing which is kind of like playing with their food. Orca will slap their prey with their tail or headbutt their meal before eating it.

Communication

Orcas produce clicks, whistles, and pulse calls. They use clicks to locate prey, navigate and interact socially. Orca family members are also known to speak in their own dialect composed of specific repetitive calls. The dialect is learned through orca mothers and other pod members. This family language is a special way orcas maintain group identity and cohesiveness. How similar a dialect is, can reflect the degree of relatedness between pods.

Great White Shark Versus the Orca

Great white sharks don't come close to rivaling orcas based on size. A great white shark's average length is between fifteen to twenty feet and their average weight is three tons. In comparison, the orca is between twenty-three and thirty-two feet long and weighs ten tons. In addition to their physical differences, they have major behavioral differences as well.

In 2017, beachgoers discovered the bodies of great white sharks washed up on the beaches of South Africa. The bodies ranged in size from nine feet to sixteen feet, and allegedly they all had their livers eaten out of them by orcas. Perhaps because they all work together, orcas figured out that shark liver was healthy and tasted great. Another example of this happened in 1997 when a marine biologist noticed an orca slam into a great white shark and stun the shark. This gave the orca the ability to flip the shark over, drown him and eat out its liver.

Protectors of Humans

Orcas are the social protector of humankind and were referred to as the lord of the ocean by Native Americans. Curious and always willing to explore new things, orcas have been thought to protect humans from sharks when boats are capsized. They are even known to help humans hunt whales by driving the whales towards ships in exchange for the whale's tongue. Interestingly enough, there are no reported attacks on humans in the wild, and orcas are not an endangered species, as of now.

This explains why most of us don't have much to come to mind other than Free Willy when you think about orcas. Now you're probably saying to yourself, "Ok, great Justin. Thanks for the history lesson. What the hell does this have to do with anything?"

I'm glad you asked. Turn the page and let's dive into the goal of this book.

I

Experience

In this part, you will go on a journey to learn how I collected clues from the world, and relationships with others to recognize the difference between an apex and average person.

The Goal of This Book

Why Be The Orca?

The goal of this book is to provide you with an opportunity to give yourself a deep assessment on your mindset, health, spirituality/religion, relationships, career, finances, communication—trust me this list can go on for days.

Have you been operating like an orca (apex) or a shark (alpha)? The goal of this book is to equip you with a mental arsenal to be an apex predator in your field. You'll learn how to do this in a way that doesn't involve placing fear in others, but rather allows you to have an approach with laser-like precision; an approach that doesn't cause fear but supreme respect. You can rise above the noise of the other sharks and become a true authority figure in your field whether you're an entrepreneur, corporate executive, customer service rep, flipping burgers (Beyond Beef burgers, of course), or a stay-at-home parent.

The key here is for you to be in the top one percent of the one percent. You may not be popular to the masses, you may not get all the likes or followers on social media, your videos may not go viral, you may not have a line of people at your vendor table, however, you attract the "experts," because you've positioned yourself as the authority. This isn't done in a way that's arrogant or fearful—the same way you think of a shark—but in a way where you have an acute focus, a precise approach, supreme tactics and crystal-clear communication that demands attention and respect. This lets the ten percent of experts know exactly who should be guiding them to their desired outcomes.

This information is compiled of techniques that I have used myself with climbing the ladder in the entrepreneurial streets of Charlotte, North Carolina. All I ask is that you keep an open mind. Some of what you may read may go against your beliefs and might even urge you to put this book down. However, I want to assure you that there is joy on the other side of the uncomfortable. With that being said, let's get started.

Senior Year

In the summer of 2006, I started to notice what separates good from great, alpha and apex. There's always that apex individual who stands above all the rest. For me, a young teenage basketball player, the apex predator in the basketball world was Kobe Bryant.

I didn't have Kobe's talent or skill, however, I noticed what burned inside Kobe wasn't just his talent for basketball, but his intelligence. I studied how his eyes would change during the heat of the basketball game, and I would say to myself, I need to develop *that*. I didn't know exactly what *that* was so I had to train.

I didn't grow up the best basketball player. As a matter of fact, I wasn't good at all when I first started, so I would practice my game as much as I could. When I was twelve years old, my uncle Herb took me and my cousin Trey to the YMCA at 5 a.m. every morning during Christmas break. The first time he did it, I was a bit upset that he woke us up that early to play basketball. Little did I know that he was planting a seed in me and teaching me to recognize what it took to be better than everyone else.

That's when I fell in love with training and practicing to better myself.

The summer of my senior year, there was this guy at the YMCA who used to always workout. When I asked him if he could train me, he said, "Sure. Be here at 5 a.m." I thought, I hope he doesn't think that's going to be hard for me to do. I always heard how the best players woke up real early to train, so I knew this was just a part of the process to be great.

We trained for a few months and I can tell I'm getting better. I'm doing things I never could do before, and picking things up fast. So when school comes, I know I'll be ready to do whatever it takes to win.

Once school starts, however, things take a different turn. The coach and I didn't have the best relationship, and to prove a point, he cut me from the basketball team. That was definitely devastating, but not compared to what would come next. One day during tryouts, I come home and my mom is crying, and I don't understand what's going on. She tells me we have to move and that the house was in foreclosure.

All of the sudden, my life shifts in just a couple of weeks. Not only was I cut from the basketball team and we were forced to move, but I would be looking for another school to attend. We moved around different times to stay with several of my mom's friends until my mom told me that we will be staying with my grandfather. That's when we decided I would transfer to West Charlotte High School.

It was at West Charlotte where I noticed different types of alpha and apex personalities. At West Charlotte, I noticed a different culture. It was nothing like my previous high school, Garinger. West Charlotte had a culture much like the rest of America, centered around status, just a different type of status. Who had the most girls, who had the latest Js (Jordans), who dressed the best, who was the most street, best in sports, who could crack the most jokes, who was having the most sex, who was the smartest. It was mainly about who had the most respect and who was popular.

The school was a unique blend of students. The people I was hanging out with seemed to be at the top of the social hierarchy in school.

I was always on the lookout to see who stood out the most, who was the best all-around student. I didn't even realize back then what an apex predator was, but I always knew there was someone who stood out from the pack. *That* was my ultimate goal in life—stand out from the pack. I looked for the same characteristics in others.

For instance, Kobe Bryant, even while he was well known at the time, most of the country wasn't a big fan of him. However, experts and players respected him on the court.

In the boxing world, Floyd Mayweather was the same. Casual boxing fans would think he was just one fight away from being knocked out and his career over. However, again the experts knew he was the authority of the ring. I always wanted to study both the authority figures and those whose contributions were overlooked in their industry. Those who possessed certain talents and skills that couldn't be seen by the untrained eye.

In my mind, there was no need to do what everyone else was doing.

* * *

At West Charlotte, it seemed like we went to parties every weekend. Since we lost our home, and my mom was away at seminary school in Virginia every weekend, I stayed with my friend, Freddie Perdue. I say friend, however, Freddie was like my little brother.

Freddie knew where all the parties were, had all the girls and Jordans for every day of the week. Freddie was a track star recruited by Division I schools and was highly intelligent. One of Freddie's overlooked talents was playing chess. He was a national-ranked chess player in high school, which didn't seem like much, however it was something he was known for.

Most of the parties we went to were in run down clubs, random spaces and house parties. Nine times out of ten, they ended in shootouts. We often threw caution to the wind and said, fuck it. Whatever happens, happens.

We'd been going out and it was a lot of us. Travonta, Quay, BuBu, Freddie, Shaul, JJ, Mike Little, Desmond, Reese, Harry. Most of the guys were interchangeable, however this was like our core nucleus who always partied every weekend. We had a lot of close run-ins with trouble.

Then one night something happened. It was February 16, 2007 when one of my classmates who I'd never partied with came out with us. His name was Travis Moore, and I noticed something different about him. The fellas reacted totally different to Travis than everyone else. Not out of fear, but another level of respect. It was on this weekend I learned just who Travis Moore was.

The first time I met Travis was the day I transferred to West Charlotte. He was in my gym class. My purpose for coming to West Charlotte was to play basketball. I was recruited through MySpace by Freddie. We're playing basketball in class when I go up for a lay-up and ironically get my shot blocked by someone like 5'5". Everyone in the gym was oooing and aahhhing.

I learned two things in that moment: I can't take no one at this school for granted playing basketball, and I learned exactly the kind of person Travis was.

He looked at me and said something like:

"Fuck that shit. Keep ballin', bruh."

And that's exactly what I did.

I didn't see Travis much around school like I did most people. However, when I did, he was always smiling or making someone else smile. Mainly girls.

When he came out with us on that weekend, I was shocked. It was a typical West Charlotte Friday night at yet another typical Charlotte party. This time we were at Tuskegee Recreation Center, also known as the Tuck Rec Center.

Interestingly enough, even at this party Travis was the center of attention. The spotlight usually was on Freddie, because he was a good dancer.

This party ends like most parties in Charlotte, back in those days. A fight breaks out, someone starts shooting in the parking lot, and you find yourself getting low, dodging bullets and rushing to the car to go home.

The next day we're relaxing and getting ready for a good follow-up party on Saturday night. That would be the perfect way to end the weekend before going back to school on Monday. But this Saturday night party was a little different than the rest. It seemed like everyone from West Charlotte, and students from other schools came out as well. Travis, of course, was out too.

This party was in a small apartment. Everything was so crammed that your senses are heightened and you are more aware of what's happening even if it's in the dark. Usually at these parties, someone with us was getting some type of attention. It was either Bubu, who was possibly about to fight someone, or Freddie, who might be dancing in the middle of the crowd. However this time it seemed like everyone's attention was on our whole crew. The apartment was on the East Side, and most of us lived on the West Side, particularly Beatties Ford Road. Not saying this we had beef with this neighborhood, but parties bring different energy out of people.

So there we were in this small, packed apartment. I don't really know how many of us were in there. The music is playing, the girls are dancing, some weed is getting smoked, and sadly enough we're even drinking alcohol. Then we leave, to meet up with some of our friends at the McDonald's up the street. I mean the party was cool but for our standards it was kind of weak.

We drive up the street to meet some more people and what was once a three or five car caravan is now pushing ten or more. I really don't know how many people were in each car. I believe I even saw some people sitting up on top of each other.

Once we get back to the party, the atmosphere was definitely different than before. Not only because of the extra people we brought back, but it was a much different crowd at the apartment complex too. We started seeing more dudes outside. Some are showing their faces. Some have hoodies on. Naturally they came for the girls. However this is Charlotte, which means they came for drama as well.

All of this was nothing new, to be perfectly honest. Just another Saturday night. Back inside, the party is the same as before. The music's playing, girls are dancing, weed is being smoked, people are drinking. This time, a small ruckus is going on outside. I instantly ask, "Where's Bubu?"

At that same time I overhear Travis ask Quay the same thing.

"He's outside," Quay says.

"With who?" Travis asks.

"Justin."

"Justin who?" Travis asks. "From the other school?"

"Yes."

Then Travis says something I couldn't even believe.

"That's not our Justin," he says. "Because Big Justin won't let anything happen to Bubu."

For a moment I was like, what the hell did I just hear? Not in a bad way. In my mind, Bubu could hold his on. He's been doing this for quite some time now. What really stood out to me the most was that Travis had that much trust in me. I'd arrived at West Charlotte in November of 2006 and Travis had only known me for three months. It shocked me how much he trusted me, someone he'd only known at the most for ninety days. It was that night I learned Travis viewed the world very differently from most people.

Things at the party get a little back to normal (whatever that means). Bubu came back inside, the party starts to get crunk (2007 slang that means it's reaching its peak). Then the song of the year by DG Yola "I Ain't Gon Let Up" starts playing. This song is a party changer. Hands go in the air, but I'm not talking about high fives. I mean gang signs and people are reppin' their neighborhood or their side of town. Again, this is nothing new.

We start hearing Bloods say what they say. Our crew gets louder than usual yelling "BEATTIES FORD!" Someone even yelled out, "FUCK Y'ALL NIGGAS! WE FROM DA FORD!"

By the time we get to the second verse of the song people are rocking to the music, jumping, shoving, throwing up signs and reppin' where they were from. When DG Yola says "I JUST DON'T GIVE A FUCK!" We hear a loud POP.

The music was so loud, and it happened so quick it could have been a balloon popping. But then we hear it again. We immediately knew shots were being fired into the crowd. We tried to find a space to get low in this tiny apartment crammed full of people. Once I realized none of us were shot, I started thinking, the minute this is over I'm heading to the car.

The lights flashed on and all that changed. It seemed like the room got bigger and everything was happening in slow motion. Someone's hand was stretched out for help and blood was everywhere. I saw the look in their eyes and they locked eyes with me. I realized I know them.

Travis was shot.

When I saw him on the ground I dropped to my knees and thought about how was I going to keep him alive. I told him, "You're going to be OK, just believe it. You'll come back to school, and we'll go on like nothing happened."

I wasn't the only person thinking how to save him. Quay, Freddie, Mike Little, Reese (Maurice), Desmond, Bubu, Harry, and even Rara (Lamont) were trying to figure it out too. We were all teenagers. All kids. Bubu was in the living room so angry he was throwing a fit. I think Freddie tried to calm him down and that didn't end too well.

The woman who rented the apartment asked if we could calm him down. I looked over at him and said "he'll be 'aight. He's not the one shot, and he isn't hitting Travis."

I was hoping for the best, but I noticed blood forming in the front of Travis's mouth. I took my shirt to remove what seemed to be a clot, because I didn't want him to stop breathing. I don't know if that helped or not. I was just doing the best I could at the time. It was at that moment I saw a different look in Travis' eyes.

At first he was looking at me. Then it was like he was looking *through* me. A feeling came over me that I didn't want to accept, but I was still keeping hope alive. Even at this moment, I told myself, *anything is possible. Travis could make it out of this.* Remember this anything is possible mentality for later parts of the book.

When the police and paramedics arrived, we all moved aside, and it felt like I stepped back into the regular universe, because in that apartment, time had stopped. Outside some were in shock, frozen, and some were going crazy. At one point a police officer approached me and said, "You seem to be the only one under control. Could you please calm your friends down?" In my head I'm thinking, just how the fuck am I supposed to do that? I'm two seconds away from doing something crazy myself.

"Uhh sure," I said.

I looked up and they were putting Travis in the ambulance. I remember telling people to get in a car with whoever they felt like riding with and go. I got in my car along with Freddie, Travonta, and Harry. I remember following the paramedics as fast as I could, running every red light they ran just to make it to the hospital at the same time as the paramedics.

I was driving so fast I ended up going to the wrong hospital. When I got

11

to the right hospital, I made it just in time to see them take Travis inside the emergency room. We stood around a few hours until we were told to go home and wait for more news.

We all went to Freddie's house and sat down and cried. We each had our own reflections of what happened. Travonta texted his girlfriend who's mom worked at the hospital. She told us that Travis didn't make it. Travis died Sunday morning February 18, 2007 at the age of seventeen.

Now, it wasn't until after Travis's death that I realized just how much of an orca he was. That Sunday night, we all met at Travis's sister's place to share our memories about the time we spent with him. When I looked at the walls in his room, I saw a very different picture of who he was.

Travis had all his report cards□like enough to make a stack of them□all hung up on his wall with thumb tact. I looked at them and saw that he had no less than a 3.5 GPA on every report card. When I saw that, I thought to myself, damn I didn't know he was that smart.

Travis wanted to go to the University of North Carolina to be a doctor or something in the medical field. I later found out Travis had gone to Germany because of his good grades and studied different cultures. While most of us his age were busy playing around, Travis was making a name for himself on an international level.

Remember what we discussed earlier about the orca being an apex predator because of its intelligence? Travis also had a very positive attitude and a smile that changed everyone he came in contact with. He didn't have to fit in. His attitude made him stand out whenever he wanted. I later found out that Travis could have any girl in the school and possibly did.

Another reason I hardly saw Travis on the weekends was because he worked at a shoe store called Athlete's Foot. Now, it's not uncommon for teens to work, however to me it just added to the brilliance of who Travis Moore was.

At his candlelight vigil people from all different walks of life paid their respects to Travis. Many said kind powerful words about his life and his impact on them. It was then I realized Travis was the apex predator of West Charlotte. He wasn't crazy popular, however Travis was at the top of the food chain. He was the top one percent of the one percent, and he was the first orca I ever met. He was intelligent, had all the girls, different Jordan sneakers for every day. He was charismatic, hard-working, well-traveled, played football, had a smile and sense of humor. At the young age of seventeen, he got respect from everyone who he met. He lived life to its full potential and on his own terms.

* * *

By June 2007, I walked the stage to receive my diploma from West Charlotte High School. As I walked to sit back down, my friend Jamaal Miller says, "Shoulder thang, do the bank head bounce."

It felt so great to graduate, because I barely made it through school that year. It wasn't because of grades. It was because of attendance. I skipped school because I just wasn't into it as much as I used to be. I knew I would pass, I was just ready for it to be over with so I could close that chapter of my life and move on to college.

A&T

Ever since eleventh grade, I knew I was going to attend North Carolina Agriculture & Technical State University. My cousin Trey took me there for the first time and I never stopped visiting for years afterward.

I never went to college with the plan of starting a professional career or future. For me, college was a chance to leave some of the trauma from Charlotte behind—especially from my senior year. My freshman year in college all I could think about was dorm rooms and freedom. That was it.

Luckily enough 70 percent of Charlotte was already attending A&T so it wasn't going to take long for me to meet people I knew or could relate to. As a matter of fact, I travelled to A&T my senior year so much that I met a decent amount of people prior to starting college.

Antwon Townsend, known as Twon, was my friend and classmate from Garinger High, who also was at A&T. Twon introduced me to the people who would end up being my daily crew: Lavonte Kendrick, Silas Ross and Andre Russell. A few other people I knew before arriving were Moe, Khalil, Barry and my cousin Trey.

Freshman year was cool. I noticed so many cultures on campus. People were from all over the country. You had people from down South, the Midwest, up North and it seemed every culture was jockeying for position.

I started to notice cultural influences, such as the clothes people wore, the type of slang they used, their attitude and demeanor. It was one big melting pot of people, which breeds constant competition for status, sex, fashion, money, and intelligence. Only this was on an entirely different level.

14

My freshman year was when I kind of realized I didn't know where I fit in. I didn't feel I could relate with most of the students because I didn't see college as the turning point of my life. It was just something to do at the time. So I did what most would do, just go through the motions and hope for the best.

My first semester was pretty cool. The crew I hung out with was pretty well known. We always hung out at Aggie Suites. These dudes were older than me, so I pretty much sat back and watched them interact with all the upperclassmen. Again I ended up in a crew where everyone is damn near a ladies man, and I'm thinking, damn this amazing.

During that first semester, I got a taste of the Thursday night college club scene. It was like watching a scene straight from a music video. Just a bunch of college students living out their best life, I guess. I used to have the time of my life at the club, lots of underage drinking and a lot of night food from Cook Out, a burger and barbecue place.

On the weekends, there would be an even bigger party, house parties mainly—only difference was that most of these parties didn't end in violence. For the most part, they dwindled down until everybody decided to go home. I can't recall hardly any ending with gunshots or anything like that, which was a relief.

To this day I can't tell you what it was like to do homework my first semester. I know I was part of a few study groups, but actually sitting down and doing homework or studying for exams? I couldn't give you the slightest insight.

My first semester was a test for me to get used to the idea of life on my own and understand my level of responsibility. I also learned about this quest of mine to be the best at whatever I chose to do. I didn't choose to do much of anything at that time. I was just going in circles not truly knowing what to pay attention to when it came to my career.

I came to realize why I hung around my friends. You may not understand it when you're young—to be honest you can be older and not realize it until you read this book—but you are connected to everyone you encounter, and more importantly, with the people with whom you associate.

One night, Vonte, Twon, Silas, Barry, Andre and I were sitting around Silas and Barry's room. We started discussing our past and how we grew up as children. We all came from similar yet different backgrounds. On this night in particular, we all realized we had a common bond. I'm not too sure how this conversation started, nor am I certain on every detail, but I remember us talking about either growing up without seeing our fathers, him not being involved (even if he was actively there), or just having a damaged relationship with our fathers. It was at that moment I realized most of us were learning by going off of instincts or influences. We were trying to become a man in a world where our own fathers weren't present to show us how to do so.

When a child doesn't have their parent, they naturally don't have a part of themselves. I learned we all had taken on the responsibility of a father/husband persona in our households, even while we were still teens. Now that I'm thirty years old, I can say we were still kids even during that conversation, wondering why things never truly added up. We didn't know we were trying to take on a position that wasn't naturally meant to be fulfilled. It was like trying to fit a round circle in a square peg, only we didn't see it that way.

I realized on this night why I hung out with the people I did. I started noticing the hidden variables that influence our lives. We didn't know it then, but we had just created a bond that was going to last for a long time.

Exams

During my first semester at school, I noticed how things changed when it got closer to semester exams. People's attitudes and focus changed a lot. It was a big switch, and it was definitely contagious to say the least. Most were studying in their dorms, some in the library, some in their apartments, but everywhere you looked the focus for exams was real. This was a real difference between college and high school.

In high school I never thought twice about really studying for exams, because I knew I was going to pass when it was all said and done. Plus high school was free, but in college, you have to pay or are on scholarship. We all know when you add money to any situation the speed and effort you apply amplifies a bit, or at least it should.

Exams for me were pretty good. I know I didn't have outstanding grades or a crazy GPA that semester otherwise I'd be able to tell you exactly how they turned out. All I can say for this semester is I noticed a sudden shift in my focus and attitude.

When exams were over, it's like the entire campus let out a sigh of relief at the same time. Before, everyone was tense, anxious and some were so worried their face was almost changing colors. Afterward, you could see some smiles and a light in their face. They didn't know if they passed or not, but they were just happy that the moment of discomfort was over.

Orca Moment: If you pay attention to the world around you, you'll notice how the majority of people seem to operate on the same wavelength. Not saying it's all bad, nor is it all good. Just take small mental notes and allow life to show you what it means later.

With the semester coming to a close, students were about to go on their first college break, get back home and have a grand experience catching up with family or friends from high school. Some might even connect with people they met in college.

I did some of that, but for the most part me and my mom were still moving. When you move from house to house, you end up accumulating a lot of things, and the clutter ends up taking a toll on you in the long run. I loved being home, however reality was hard to overcome. We moved into what you call a fixer-upper and with the financial situation we were in at the time, the fixing-up phase just kept getting pushed back and pushed back. In some ways it gave me motivation to do two things: Go back to school and try to do well enough to one day change my financial situation. Or make money immediately.

For me, going back to Charlotte was just more observation than anything. I noticed the difference in how the environment shifted between college and being home. At times, I felt like I was on the outside looking in. The conversations and energy was different, however the focus remained the same. At that time, I was just figuring out where I wanted to go next in life and how to get there.

The Greatest Homecoming on Earth

Now, I know everyone has their own reason for wanting to attend A&T, however, no matter what anyone tells you, one of those reasons is for homecoming. A&T's homecoming was known as The Greatest Homecoming on Earth or GHOE. I know it's the main reason *I* wanted to go to the school. When most people think of GHOE, they only think of Friday festivities, the football game on Saturday, walking on the yard, and concerts and parties going around all over the city of Greensboro.

When you're a student, homecoming week on campus is an entirely different experience all together. For the entire week leading up to homecoming, the campus is filled with events. Some are for fun, like a comedy show in the gym, and some were for networking purposes. You get to meet up with alumni who share their knowledge and may even mentor you. They might assist you in furthering your career.

I'm sad to say I didn't really participate in any of those types of activities for homecoming. As I stated in the beginning, I was just going to college to get away, enjoy time on my own and enjoy homecoming, of course.

During homecoming week, the only thing everyone —and I do mean *everyone*—was talking about is what they were going to wear for Saturday. Now, mind you, I'm from Charlotte, and what I considered fly back then was some nice jeans, an LRG shirt and some clean shoes.

It wasn't until I met Silas Ross that all that changed. Back then, possibly still until this very day, Silas could have been not just a model, but a spokesman for the Ralph Lauren clothing line. I mean, it got so serious with Silas he even had Ralph Lauren socks to match certain polo shirts. That was all he wore. Trust me when I say Ralph Lauren was a way of life for Silas.

As I said, college was a clash of different cultures and styles. As a freshman who just turned eighteen years old, I was really trying to figure out what my place would be. As it got closer and closer to homecoming weekend, I still hadn't decided what I would wear. All the outfits I had in my head were gone by the time I got to the mall, so I decided to take the Silas approach. I went to the Ralph Lauren store and purchased a brown shirt with light brown stripes and some brown dress pants. I had a pair of my only black dress shoes ready, and I decided that was going to be my outfit for Saturday.

I figured homecoming my freshman year was either a blast or it was a complete waste of time. I can't actually recall much of what I did, which gives you an idea of the bulk of my college experience. I do remember receiving different looks from females, as if they approved of the switch in wardrobe.

In my head I started thinking, OK, Silas, you may be on to something.

That experience taught me that appearance was everything and that the majority of people build a perception about you based off how you present yourself. Not only did Silas show me that, but Vonte did as well. Now I'm not saying I learned the lesson immediately right away, but it was something I started paying attention to.

I wanted to purchase as many nice clothes as I could see, and at times would go buy a little here and there. Even though I was in college and left certain things behind in Charlotte, the truth was that my finances were always in my face. We'll get to that later in this chapter.

Second Semester

Second semester was a little different. I had gotten my feet wet, got over a major hurdle of the first semester of college, and in my mind was headed into the home stretch of completing my freshman year of college.

Over the years, I noticed I traditionally didn't do things well my first time learning something. In the case of A&T, I was learning the ebb and flow of college. Picking up on certain variables, whether internal or external, are key to human survival. The brain is always looking for something familiar and this second semester of college was no different.

I had a totally different outlook than I did when I first arrived. I felt more focused on two things: grades and money. Only one of the two did I see some type of immediate change-money.

Coming back from the break, I noticed all the people who got new things for the holidays. Of course, you have to come back to school and show it off, right? Some got new electronic gadgets, new clothes or new vehicles. I'd be wrong to say I didn't feel like I was missing out or thinking like, damn I'd like to have some new stuff. It started to become visible that even though we are all on the same campus, there were different classes of people.

This second semester also meant way more parties. The winter was about to end, which meant everyone would be thawing out from the cold and getting warmed up for the spring. This was also the time of the year I started taking a heavy interest in smoking weed.

Once the second semester was underway, I knew right away I was going to start applying my newfound focus on grades and money. When it came to grades, I immediately found the benefit of having a study partner who was an upperclassmen☐or in this case an upperclasswoman.

See, hanging out with older people in college had its perks. Of all the people Twon, Silas, Vonte, and Roe had introduced me to, only a few of the people were studying my same major. One person, in particular, was even in a few of the same classes with me. Her name was Whitney.

Whitney was a friend of our friend, Crystal. We but we used to Crystal Pam—like Pam on the show *Martin*. Whitney and I had several classes with each other, and I always noticed she had the answer to damn near all the questions in every class. It was almost like she had taken all these classes before.

Now me being me, I think, go ask Whitney for help. So one day I asked what may have been the weirdest question for a college student to ask another college student. I asked Whitney if she could teach me how to study. Most of the time in high school, and even before, I rarely studied. I never found the need to study. Plus the way studying was taught growing up in those days was so damn boring.

To my surprise, Whitney said, "Sure, Shoulders." That was a major hurdle for me because Whitney and I had probably three classes together that semester. Per the great advice from Vonte, I chose four classes to take that semester all between the times of 10 a.m.-12 p.m. Vonte's logic around scheduling was simple: Choose a class between those times, because if it snows you'll automatically know you won't have class for that day. Now, that may seem a bit slackerish, however, it let me know Vonte paid attention to a different wave frequency of life. We'll dive deeper into that later on.

Back to studying with Whitney. The beauty in all of this is that I asked her this question early in the semester, right before spring. I figured by doing that I'll have the entire semester to learn this skill of studying which would then help me move toward having higher marks at the end of the year.

Whitney taught me all the tricks and strategies she used when she studied. Sometimes she would use music, or have something playing in the background so she could remember a certain part. It was a combination of traditional methods and using her own rhythm. At times she would go the traditional route, but overall Whitney found a way to make studying work for her. During that time, that was something I knew I desperately needed.

A lot of things started to become a new norm for me. I started to hang out more with my cousin Trey whose roommates were Moe (DJ Moezzy), Kahlil, and Niko. All were people from Charlotte who I knew before coming to school.

It wasn't as if I didn't hang with them at all, however the second semester was a bit different. I had already experienced what it was like to hang out on campus, but I noticed how different the environment was off campus. Being off campus brought more freedom. You appeared more mature, and that meant more girls, to be honest. Well, to me it did anyway.

Most of the time we would all just chill, play Xbox, or PlayStation during the week, but on the weekends things would go crazy. At first we would go to our homeboy Quis's house to party. Eventually, though, Trey and Moe decided to have parties at their apartment.

See, throwing parties wasn't a foreign thing to Trey, Moe or even me. Back when I was in eleventh grade, Trey and Moe were freshmen in college. One day they asked me a question I'm glad I said yes to. When my mom would go to Virginia every weekend for school, I would usually hang with them, go for a joy ride in the car, or just do nothing at the house. But one day in December 2005 things were different.

Trey and Moe approached me like some CIA agents.

"Bruh, we know your mom goes out of town every weekend," they said. "You down if we throw a party at your house while she's gone?"

I'm sixteen years old at the time so my answer was, hell yeah!

That night, Moe became a DJ, and he's now known by the name DJ Moezzy. That night also set the tone for more parties to come, not just that year, but in college as well.

Somewhere down the line, we learned some business skills. We charged people to enter the house party. I don't remember the price, but I know I received some "gate money," and cut some deals for folks to come in through the garage. We hired security as well. This dude from the YMCA, who was built like an NFL linebacker, did the job.

It was a great time until we forgot to clean up and my mom found out what we did the next day. She was pretty easygoing, but at that moment Trey and I were just frozen with fear. All she asked is that we clean the entire house like some maids and that was the end of it.

Now that you are caught up with a little bit of history, let's get back to college. Trey, Moe, Khalil and Niko stayed in an apartment off campus called Campus Courtyard 2. This building was very special. This is where I start to notice the real advantages of living off campus. Which increased my desire to make more money, do better in school and have my own place.

What happened at Campus Courtyard 2 was just an introduction to what was to take place the following school year. At the time, things were pretty cool and calm. I just enjoyed hanging out, and I started to become cool with Trey's roommate Khalil, who was also known as "K" or Fuller. When I found out his last name was Fuller, I cracked jokes using the line from the movie *Home Alone*, when Kevin's (Macaulay Culkin) mom told him he'd have to share a bed with his cousin, and he said, "I don't want to sleep with Fuller. He wets the bed." Ever since then, I was cool with Fuller.

One thing I admired about Fuller was that he was a constant hustler. I'll never forget when the movie *American Gangster* came out in the movie theaters. Fuller was the only person I knew at A&T, or even Greensboro for that matter, who had it on DVD already. He sold it to people for five dollars.

It was at that moment I noticed the hustle/entrepreneur spirit he possessed and that I wanted it for myself, especially during a time in my life where everything around me was going so crazy financially. At times, I was so broke I would sneak food from the cafeteria and bring it back to my dorm to eat later. I'm not sure if we were even supposed to do that, but I had to do what I had to do.

Orca Moment: *One thing to note at this moment was how Fuller*

*took full advantage of what was hot and immediately implemented a
game plan to take advantage of it. Like my coach always says, speed of
implementation is a key to success.*

Second semester was full of ups and downs. At one point, me and the guys
from Aggie Suites were hanging out in Vonte's dorm. As usual, we had
been drinking when we heard some noise outside the hallway. I really don't
remember how this started, but all I know is a fight broke out. One of my
friends was in a bad position. It looked like the other guy was going to try
some UFC shit on him. He had his hands on the back of my friend's head
ready to knee him in the face. It seemed like it all happened in slow motion,
because that's when I just punched the dude in the face. Then, his cousin
asked me what I still believe to this day was the dumbest question ever asked
during a fight:

"Why did you punch my cousin?" he asked.

"It's a fight, dumbass!" I answered.

So then me and him square up. In the beginning, it was going in my favor,
and I remember landing some good clean punches. Then out of nowhere,
this dude turns into Ray Lewis and tackles my ass, and I'm thinking, man
what the fuck just happened? I cover up, but he gets a few punches in until
Twon comes up and knocks him upside the head.

I know I definitely caught the worst of the exchange, however that night
let me know who my true friends were. Not saying something unfortunate
as fighting has to show you who your friends are, but friends rise to the
occasion for one another. That night was no different. That was the only
fight we had together as a group.

* * *

The spring at A&T was full of life. Silas, Vonte, Twon and I went to Myrtle
Beach for spring break which was a cool experience. This was also when

25

I attended my first ever—and to this day *only*—all-white party. The hype around that party was similar to an A&T homecoming. Everyone was trying to figure out what to wear or how to dress and impress someone who had been curving them the entire year.

One of the ultimate highlights of my second semester was the fact that my studying with Whitney was actually paying off. I don't actually remember taking any exams or doing much homework, however I do remember at the end of the semester I made the dean's list.

Making the dean's list wasn't necessarily a goal of mine, however it was the result of good practices, and surrounding myself with the correct people who took their education seriously.

Orca Moment: Remember when I said in the beginning orcas travel in pods and speak in their own dialect? The lesson here is that it's not a problem if you don't know how to do something or achieve a certain result. When you find the people who have already acquired what you want, and the two of you align well, then connecting with that person is your best bet to achieving your goals. Even if it seems uncomfortable in the beginning, remember you aren't there to feel comfortable. You are there to grow and growth always comes with growing pains.

I'm very thankful for Whitney, because not only did she help me make the dean's list, but she gave me the confidence that I could succeed at whatever I truly put my mind to.

At the beginning of the semester, I had two main things I wanted to focus on: grades and money. Seeing that I made the dean's list, it's safe to say I checked grades off my list. A different reality set in, however, once I realized that it still didn't change my financial situation; I was still broke. Grades were good to set you up for future success, however I needed money now.

During summer break, I decided to set some goals for myself: Work as much as possible, save money to get my own apartment and not worry about where money was coming from. Or so I thought.

Sophomore Summer

The summer of my sophomore year in college was one of the biggest turning points in my life. My entire goal that summer was to work and save my money. There were so many things I wanted that I didn't know where to start. Where I lived on Beatties Ford Road in Charlotte, everybody was making money off of something. I was torn between getting a job and hustling until my mom said she had someone who would hire me. I would work at Carolina Medical Center, known as Atrium Health today. I told her great, I'll do it. She said all you have to do is pass a drug test. I gave her the most honest smile ever while in the back of my head thinking, damn, how in the hell am I going to do that?

Immediately, I did all I could to flush my system. I'd just left school so I definitely had weed in my system. The question was, how long would it take for me to clean it out? I did everything I could from drinking insane amounts of water to playing basketball like three times so I could break a sweat. I even went so far as buying some cleaner to flush it out. One thing was for sure: I needed this damn job.

The day came for my drug test. I think I recited every religious prayer I could think of to pass this test. I walked inside, filled out the application-or whatever the process was back in 2008-and they finally gave me The Cup. I grabbed it with a confident smile on my face, went to the bathroom and prayed everything would work out.

The next few weeks were the longest weeks of my entire life. Finally, I got a notice that said I got the job. I was so happy not just because I got a job, but because I could also smoke weed again.

Soon after that, I had another opportunity. My friend told me how he got a job at Autobell and they were barely doing drug testing. They did a swab test and all I did was stick a swab under my tongue and was good to go. I got that job too.

By the summer of 2008, I had two jobs and I'm thinking, I am on my way to have some money this summer. The only thing I did that entire summer was work. I worked at the hospital and sometimes when I got off I would go straight to Autobell. I did this almost every day. Back and forth, every day, every day, every day, every day. I was working so much that I didn't get to work out. I went to play some basketball and, in a very tragic moment, actually almost broke my ankle. That same summer I got elbowed in the lip. It was busted so bad that the next morning I woke up with blood on my teeth. I almost considered myself retired from basketball that summer.

The thing I learned from working every day was that there was still something missing. I realized I wasn't making enough money, because I hadn't changed anything about my financial predicament. I didn't know how. The only thing I did was go to work, get a check, spend it and do it all over again.

That summer was a fun one. I went to see Gucci Mane for the first time in Greensboro, drove around a lot and smoked a lot of weed as well.

Orca Moment: *I didn't know it then, but I was using fun (smoking weed, driving to Greensboro etc.) to numb the fact that I knew nothing about how to actually acquire wealth or even save money. The pain of not knowing was so deep I never even knew how to consider getting educated on the subject.*

I was exposed to all of life's possibilities and ways of making money. In a sense I was working to finally be able to get something I wanted since my freshman year—my own apartment. I figured this goal would help me save money and be more responsible. In a way it did. I remember at work I would sit down at my cubicle all day and write out scenarios. I tracked everything I would need from rent money, to food, to toilet paper. I was a real maniac. I wanted that apartment so bad. It was going to be my own bit of freedom.

When my mom agreed to co-sign, it was still summertime. I wasn't moving in anytime soon, but I knew I was going to have that apartment. By the end of the summer, I'd saved a good bit of money, or at least I thought I did. I learned that working a ten-dollar-an-hour job, plus another job, wasn't going to be the ultimate gamechanger I thought it would be.

I didn't know what it took to make a good amount of money, save it and not spend it on my vices. Because of that, I worked a lot and hung out in places like Beatties Ford Road. I was doing a lot of running around and hanging out with random cliques. I was looking for ways to make money when I met a homeboy who we called Hurt. He stayed with my homeboy, Khalil. He always struck me as a person who was constantly hustling, and I started to notice the people around him were much the same. Hurt was very much a street guy. We called him an OG during that time and he still is. Only thing I really knew about the streets was violence watching my homeboy get killed and all.

That summer, me and Hurt, Khalil and Vonte would just chill, smoke weed and talk. But it wasn't until later I noticed Hurt was a totally different individual than any other person I'd ever met. We start learning things about people. Nothing bad, but just what makes them who they are. At that point in my life, I didn't know what I wanted. I didn't know whether I should continue with school or do what I felt like I was yearning to do—learn how to make more money.

Sophomore year, learning to make more money was the only thing I was focused on. I paid attention to grades, yeah a little bit, and girls of course, but I never really understood how to go to school, have a job and have other stuff. I felt in a weird predicament.

The Apartment

College life seemed like it was working out really, really well for me. I had had some money saved, had some clothes, thinking that I was going to be able to survive off that little bit of money I made. On top of that, we had something called a refund check. When you go to college and you live off campus, you get a crazy refund check. I think I learned what my refund check was before actually getting it, and that's what had me excited as well. I already had a couple thousand dollars saved up. So I figured I would put most of this toward the rent, do some other things with the money and be all good. Little did I know that plan wasn't very good.

When I finally got my first apartment, I instantly started feeling like I had a different status. People would ask if they could come over and hang out. I'd always be like, yeah, sure y'all can come over and hang out. When I found out my roommate was going to be Twon, I knew we definitely were gonna have a good time. I'd never actually lived with Twon, but I'd known him long enough to feel comfortable living with him.

I started testing out just how much status an off-campus apartment could get you. The girls did think you were more solid, more independent, more of an adult when you had your own place. People viewed you differently. You could do anything you wanted off campus. You could smoke weed, drink, have as many people over as you want.

Living off campus meant you were no longer under the protection of the school campus. So basically, you know for all intents and purposes, you're on your own. Our apartment complex was called Riverwalk. It was kind of known to be a bit ratchet as we call it, or a bit hood, but at the end of the day so was all of Greensboro. My first night I think I just had a party. It wasn't even a big party. Just everybody hanging out.

When it came time to schedule my classes, I scheduled classes so I could maximize as much time as possible in this apartment. Around the same time, I started to realize just how many "things" I wanted. Every Saturday it seemed like I would be out buying clothes. I would go buy shoes and then just hang out at the apartment. I was really stepping into this false belief of maintaining status. I was living what I thought was a life of responsibility, a life of independence being on my own. But one thing I never actually learned was how to manage money.

I was eighteen years old living in this apartment when I started to realize I probably needed to slow down on spending money. I didn't have a hustle. I didn't have anything going on outside of just going to school. My main focus, however, was getting back to that apartment, chilling, then hanging out with my friends. The apartment was right down the street from my cousin Trey's apartment and where Maurice, Nico and Khalil lived at Campus Courtyard Two.

The first semester of sophomore year—just like freshman year—the talk of the year was homecoming, homecoming, homecoming. Everybody wanted to know what you were going to do or wear for homecoming. The only difference was this year I had me a little bit of money, and I knew what I wanted to do. We ended up going to a comedy show by Mike Epps. When I say we, I mean me, Vonte, Twon and a few other guys. We also went to the concert featuring Young Jeezy, Rick Ross, T-Pain and Plies. We had company over at the apartment so I could really utilize the place.

That year, the homecoming vibes just kept going over and over with more parties. And the more they kept coming, the more I was thinking I wasn't really feeling school. I started noticing my friends were making money hustling, and that seemed to be more my thing. I'd ask myself how am I going to get some more money? What am I going to do? I knew I wasn't going to be able to rely on my mom. I didn't really want some campus job either. I really didn't even know where I wanted to work.

So the whole time I'm in college, I was masking the fact that I didn't know what I was going to do for cash. I was just having fun spending money, smoking weed, going to parties and chasing girls. But around this time after homecoming, things just started getting different. I was really searching.

Atlanta

I was at school trying to live my life and saw everyone around me living theirs. At times, I didn't really feel like I had the direction or support I needed. I started looking for people who seemed like they would support me or understand what I was going through being in college and losing a home the previous year. I really didn't feel like the people I grew up with could relate to me or they might judge me. This was just some of what was going on in my nineteen-year-old head.

When I lived in Charlotte or in Greensboro, I always saw people who were just getting wads of cash or just getting money, so I started taking a different liking to Khalil and our homeboy, Hurt. As I said before, Khalil just made a lot of money off of selling the *American Gangster* DVD while it was still in theaters. I really didn't know it then, but I was about to embark on a journey.

I felt like it was time for me to try a different type of school. The one I was in just was not fitting me. Sometimes I'd be in school and my mind would start wandering. I'd think about things I always wanted to do but never actually did. I would think about my mom telling me what was going on at home. I didn't feel like I could really contribute to my own situation.

By this time, a lot of the friends I hung out with my freshman year started blending in with the people I knew from Charlotte. As a matter of fact, we formed this intramural basketball team with Trey, Vonte, Moe, Silas and a few others. We were pretty damn good. We only lost to the traveling intramural team, and we actually all developed a different type of bond.

Some still credit me for introducing everyone to each other. I don't know if I can actually take full responsibility for that. I mean, we are at A&T and you are bound to run across somebody that somebody else might know but hey, it's pretty cool.

So again, we developed this bond, and for the most part, me and Vonte were always up at Campus Courtyard Two. Mostly we played video games, smoked weed, and watched these crazy documentaries. We watched these hood documentaries about former drug dealers. We watched a lot of stuff dealing with crime, and it really dawned on me that Hurt knew a lot about the streets. For real, like *a lot*. It was as if when we went to school, we would get our book education, and when we saw Hurt, we would get our street education. We learned the ins and outs of the streets. We learned about people, how dudes in the streets act, how to always be on guard, how to know whether or not you can recognize a predicament you are in. We learned just about the world in general.

Now, another surprising fact about Campus Courtyard Two, it was very much not your traditional college apartment. Downstairs were a few guys from the West Coast who gang banged. On the middle level were some people from Virginia and then you had us at the top level.

But it was always something going on. Too much going on for it to be a regular college campus apartment. Like, you would notice gang beef between different gangs. I remember this one weekend where me, Twon and one of our friends had a gun. We were out and about in the party scene when we almost got into a fight with a guy. He was like thirty or forty years old claiming he was a Blood hanging around college kids. This was all because Twon had a Boston Red Sox hat with the B on it. For the life of me, I couldn't really understand it. You know, this is supposed to be college. This is what I wanted to leave behind in Charlotte.

So my friend left the gun, and I picked it up ready to defend Twon.

"Yo, Twon," I said. "What is going on with this dude?"

The gun was terrible, because it would jam, but in my mind I just knew, hell this is gonna be the one shot that's gonna go off. Luckily, the situation got defused.

At A&T there were a lot of people from a certain area in Greensboro□and a lot of people from North Carolina in general who weren't students□who would come around and bring about different levels of drama. The first semester of my sophomore year was really just an eye-opener to what really goes on in other people's lives.

One of the greatest things about that fall semester was that homecoming was the same weekend as my birthday. So I turned nineteen in my own apartment during homecoming, and that was very cool. As a nineteen-year-old living on my own, out in the world learning life on the go, I started realizing I didn't have some things other people had. I didn't have real knowledge on how to manage money. I possibly ignored this growing up or maybe it was not seriously taught. No one really took the time to drill it into my head as they tried to with Christianity or doing chores or some shit.

I remember when my uncle Herb warned me about having my own apartment. He'd say things like, "Hey, you might want to take your time J," or "You might want to just wait." At that point I didn't realize what he was saying, I thought, he just didn't want to support me.

In the fall of my sophomore year, I'd never really thought about how to make my college experience better. I just wanted to move forward and get it over with. That year showed me how much discipline I didn't have and how much I did not know about the responsibility of having your own place.

Orca Moment: You never truly learn what a situation is like until you're living it. When you're in a tough situation, this is not the moment you turn around and flee. You need to realize that you can learn lessons along the way. You learn what to change for the future. You learn from your lessons.

Thanksgiving comes and I don't necessarily remember what I did. I might have hung out with Freddie and his family. Christmas break I went home as well, but I went back to school early to be in my apartment. That was the beauty of me being on my own. Twon would always come in and be like man, "What you doing man? You go clean your room." He was always being somebody's big brother. It was cool. You know, I understood his ways, but at the same time I was like, "Yo, you don't have no children yet, so let me just chill bro."

I started thinking more about Hurt and his ways. I started thinking, damn, I don't think I want to sell heroin or cocaine, but weed might be good. People would always say some of the best weed doesn't come from North Carolina, so I would have to go to other places to get the weed. That other place was Atlanta. People would always talk about how everything you wanted was in Atlanta.

Now, another thought in my head was to learn more about what we call "trapping." Back in 2008, trap music was stepping toward becoming its own genre. You would hear people rap about how much weed they had in their area or how much dope they had. To me it was almost like people saying, "Hey, come down here. We got it right now if you want. Come buy this." I heard the call and answered it. I was low on money. I knew a lot of people around me were low on money, but I want to actually change the situation.

At the start of the spring semester, I chose to continue living off of campus, and I received another refund check. This time it was a little bit bigger than before, and I knew I was going to do something totally different with it. Before this refund check came, I reached out to somebody I knew in Atlanta and asked him how much weed I could get for a certain amount of money. I knew I was going to get a lump sum of money. I remember thinking up scenarios with a few friends.

"If I go buy this weed and I sell it to y'all," I said. "We can make some money."

They were in.

I had my ideal clients, then I had to figure out how to get everything done. Luckily, we were blessed with a supreme opportunity. In January 2009, my friend, Chekeya, offered us some tickets to the Battle of the Bands in Atlanta. We all would get a free hotel room, free admission to the game, and free admission to the club. Me and Vonte's eyes lit up at the opportunity, because he knew exactly what I was going to do when I got down there. We didn't think twice.

Once we got to Atlanta, we were about to go to the Battle of the Bands, when I got a phone call from my cousin Trey.

"Someone got killed at the apartment," he said.

Instantly my mind is wondering who got killed and if it's somebody we knew. He said no, but the dude's name was Dennis. Trey said Dennis was either leaving his room or he was trying to get into his apartment when somebody walked up and shot him in the head. They killed him right in front of his own front door.

I don't really remember what I told Trey. I told him something comforting like, you know, just go inside and pray and everything will be alright. At that time I still didn't really understand how to express myself. I'm thinking, well shit, I saw my friend Travis die. I didn't see Dennis get killed. I didn't really know how to process that. I could hear in Trey's voice that it was a very scary, uncomfortable moment. I shared the news with everybody else and they all had a look on their faces and shook their heads. To this day I consider it a very sad situation, because I'm not sure if they ever found the person responsible for Dennis's murder.

After that news, we got ready to go out to what was then called the Georgia Dome. I had never gone to a Battle of the Bands event before, but it was very nice. You go inside the Georgia Dome, you see the Atlanta Falcons stadium and watch all the great historically black college bands just battling out.

We left early, went back to the hotel and started getting prepared for the Atlanta nightlife, which was a whole other level of club experience. See Atlanta's club scene was very different. I think it will always be on a different level than Charlotte, North Carolina. It was strangely well organized. I say it's strange because a lot of black club party scenes in Charlotte aren't well organized. Not only did they have metal detectors before you go inside, but they actually accepted credit cards as payment to get inside the club. That just blew my mind.

One of the clubs we went to was called Club Miami. It looked like a rundown building, but inside is where people really took partying to a whole different level.

Before that night, my only Atlanta party experience was when my cousin Courtney had a house party in the basement of his mom's house in ninth grade. That was insane as well. I think over a hundred-something people filled my aunt Tanji's basement all while she was asleep upstairs not knowing what was happening. That was the craziest party I'd ever been to until 2009.

Trap music was born in Atlanta in 2009 and was taking on its own identity. My favorite rapper at that time was Gucci Mane LaFlare. People just called him Gucci. You hear people rap about things, and you don't really know how serious they are. You don't know if they are really what we call "bout that life." But at Club Miami, I realized just how much Gucci Mane was really *that dude* in Atlanta. He was a big deal back then. What solidified his status even more was that I actually went to see him perform.

After that club experience, I went on to find people who were going to sell me weed. I'm thinking, I came down here to buy weed and that's what I intend to do. It was very strange. It was very different from all of my visits before this one. I'm usually in Atlanta for family events. This time I'm just here to buy something and leave. The purchase happened real quick. I gave the guy the money and he left. The interesting part was the drive back. I was super-focused on what was going on and paying attention to the road like I never had before. My only focus was making it back to Greensboro.

Once I made it back, it settled in on me what was taking place. I made it back to my apartment, and gave it like a day or so before doing anything. I already had like two people I knew who would be open to buy, so I started selling. I really realized just how fast weed can go when you know the correct people. At the same time, I learned another valuable lesson.

Orca Moment. *It's not about where you're going but the transformation that takes place along the way.*

While I'm selling weed to a few of my friends, I realize that just because I had more money didn't really mean I was making better decisions. It was to the point that I was just shuffling around a few dollars.

I realized the weed was definitely selling fast and I was going to need more soon. I set up another trip and it was the same process as before. When I got back to Greensboro, I would smoke a lot of weed. I would smoke every day between classes. I really never knew how truly lost out there I was. It wasn't the hustling that was getting to me, it was the mismanagement of money. After a while I only had enough money to hustle. I was able to buy some things, buy some food, pay the rent, but still something just wasn't right in my head.

After a while I started having thoughts of how to do more, get more. Then, the suppliers I knew just disappeared. I don't know if they got arrested or just quit. I'm not sure what happened. I tried to find someone in Greensboro, but it wasn't the same quality, and nothing was the afterward.

I eventually found out my main guy did get arrested, and, to be completely honest, I lost the desire to keep selling. If I was forced to be the same as everyone else selling weed, I didn't want to keep at it. To me, it was all about the quality. After a while I just stopped selling completely, and the money I did have went to pay for food, rent and gas.

My mind started spiraling. I was smoking weed and got really deep into conspiracy theories. Some might even say it was a bit of paranoia. I never understood what the thoughts were in my head. I just started seeing the world really differently. I was also reading this book called *The Hip Behold a Pale Horse*, which was about all the craziness going on in the world as a black man and how you feel like you still aren't free.

I was always one who wanted to know more, always wanted to dig deeper, and this time I found myself going down a crazy rabbit hole. It was a rabbit hole mixed with some truth and also mixed with a mental concept I constructed.

Over time, me, Vonte, K and Hurt would just chill, but I felt like I started losing it. I didn't really know what was going on in my thoughts. I didn't know if I was hallucinating. My mind was just going all over the place.

I felt like school was a big trap. For instance, I was in a class after I'd just finished smoking weed, and the professor put up a graph saying that jobs won't be available until 2015. I'm like, yo, we're set to graduate in 2011, and you are telling me jobs won't be available for years afterward? We start paying off student loans six months after graduation. Those numbers didn't add up to me and I was trying to figure out, why are we here then? When you're nineteen, you think everything your professor says is correct, and that's just what life is going to be, right? I wondered why I should even be in school? Why continuously do this?

I felt this was all a big game, and since I was getting so deep into conspiracy theories, I felt like signs were being revealed to me. Those signs seem to say, "This isn't the place for you." I thought I was probably much like other college students who felt they were wasting time at school.

I started thinking I could go back to Charlotte and do some things to probably make some money and come back to school after. This just got me real, real down. It got *real* bad. I didn't know what direction to go. A lot of my friends thought I was going crazy—which I probably was.

I started having a lot more flashbacks about my homeboy Travis. Being around the environment of Campus Courtyard Two, Greensboro and Riverwalk really didn't help either. I was in school to try to escape things that had happened in Charlotte, but the same things were happening over and over where I was at. I thought, if I have to go through all this I might as well go home.

That semester I decided to drop out of school. I wanted to embark on a new journey of figuring out how to make it in the regular world because, at the moment, attending college was not working.

Decisions

I was going through a dark time in my life before I dropped out of school. A lot of past trauma started showing up, and at that age I didn't really know how to handle it. I didn't know what was going on, and I damaged some of my relationships. That's when people started looking at me crazy. At that age, between nineteen and twenty-one years old, we were still pretty young kids. Friends don't know all that's going on in the world and want to help as best they can.

When I dropped out in the spring of 2009, I didn't really have any plans for what I was going to do. I was hustling or what they called trapping at school. That didn't work out but I figured I'd try something else to keep going. I didn't even take exams. I just didn't want to go back to school. My mind ran wild and the drugs and the drinking altered my beliefs. I didn't necessarily trust people or situations around me.

At times, I didn't know if I was hallucinating or hearing things. I sometimes thought people were playing tricks on me. It was real bad, and I never actually got any type of professional help for it. The only thing I knew to do was like, pray on it, or 'let it go' and all the other bull people say when they don't know what they're talking about.

Orca Moment: If you have any type of mental trauma and someone tells you that you got to "get over it," that's a clear indication you don't need to confide your problems to that person. They aren't uniquely qualified to handle it.

I head back home to Charlotte to try and find a way of making money. I really wanted a job, but that job quickly turned into being on the streets on Beatties Ford Road. During that time, I really didn't do much of anything but travel between Greensboro and Fayetteville, sleep on people's couches and go to parties. I didn't have any real life plans. I sold some weed here and there, worked odd jobs, but I had no plan. I was just out living life creating some type of false reality about myself that one day I would come up on some money.

I started running with a different crowd of people including one of my good friends from A&T, Chris. He was one of the few people I knew who lived on Beatties Ford Road who I was already really cool with. Beatties Ford Road is full of different cliques based on where you lived, people you grew up with or just chose to hang out. One group in particular was called the Wreck Boys. For the most part, they were just like everyone else trying to find ways to survive. I'm not condemning what they did in the streets, because in moments like that, you don't know what else to do. Your mind is so focused on one situation, you feel there are no other options. I felt the same.

I didn't really know how to relate to anyone else outside of folks from Beatties Ford Road. Yes, I went to school, and it was cool, but I didn't finish school, and I really didn't know what else to do. It wasn't really cool to me to just keep going to class and still struggle for money.

I decided to be on the Ford on a daily basis. This time it was a little bit different than just selling weed. I always knew you could come up on money big in the streets. I saw it all around me, and I said to myself, I got to be smart enough to get money in the streets. Period.

It was all about finding the right people, knowing who to run with or who knew what. But over time, I just kept getting caught up in more and more stuff. So that whole 2009 I spent my time praying for a lick or, as we say, praying for a big sum of money.

I tried to apply for jobs. One time I had a job working in a warehouse and caught the worst migraine ever. I never went back. I told myself at the time, it ain't for me. I ain't going to do that.

By spending all this time on The Ford, I was hanging out with friends of the family. All we would do was sit around, drink beer and smoke weed. No real direction. No real ambition. Just living. Just existing.

I really didn't know it, but I was truly lost. I was lost in the sauce of life. Lost my focus on reality and how to effectively bounce back. My focus was so limited on how to just get cash, get cash that I didn't know there was a way to build myself up.

Me and my friend would sometimes ride around looking for a lick, or looking for a come up, a way to sell some weed, borrow some money and pay it back. To be all the way honest, I was just living in a complete circle of nothingness. At the same time, I wanted to build me a name on The Ford, outside of the name I already had. While trying to do this, however, I ran into multiple situations.

Some I felt comfortable and in, some I didn't. While in the streets on my hiatus from school, I wanted to go other places in the world to see how people do live all over the world, thinking that meant something. I'd travel, meet up with girls in different neighborhoods, hoping for a different outcome to my current situation. Then I noticed it's all the same thing. I said to myself, well damn, how come everybody seems to be in the same predicament that I'm in?

What I didn't realize was that I was attracting the reality I was experiencing. Every time I would look for a new woman to date, maybe someone who could support me coming out of my situation, they would be in the same predicament as me. I was attracting who I was.

Orca Moment: *I attracted who I was. You always attract who you are being.*

I tried everything to change what I was experiencing. I tried selling weed, I even considered selling cocaine. I attempted a type of credit card hustle.

43

See at that point in time I was just about getting a dollar. I wasn't really about business. I was chasing. I wasn't building, and chasing and only being about money will lead you into a predicament that's hard to escape. Chasing the money and trying to be something I wasn't, is what led me to the worst decision I ever made.

Indicted

During my first full year out of college in the real world, all of my decisions were based upon a false persona. I started noticing that I have yet to do anything substantial. I couldn't find a job and was still out and about on the streets. I was just really lost. Just hoping and praying for something to happen.

I had to go through a lot of different ups and downs financially. I was always in a cycle of having zero money in the bank or owing money, and that was just the worst for me. The final straw was driving to Gastonia to see somebody and my car broke down. I thought, man, it really just can't get any worse than this. I'm in Gastonia and my car breaks down. I think my mom came to get me. My next thought was, now what the hell am I going to do?

Prior to that I'd heard talk from a friend of a friend about being able to come up on some money by doing a home invasion. Before then, I brushed off the idea, but now I was entertaining it. I told myself, you know what, hell, let's go for it. We talked about what we would do, and we talked about what was supposed to be in there.

The night of our plan, I went to my friend's house to pick them up. We already had an accomplice at the place we were going. Once we got in there, we had the resident at gunpoint and somebody was yelling, "Where's the money?!"

This was never done with the intention to really hurt or kill anyone. We just came for some money, some electronics, whatever valuables. All I wanted was cash. Lo and behold, while we were doing this, I started realizing that, nothing was in there. This had to be one of the worst decisions I made in my life.

"Yo, I'm leaving," I say. "I'm leaving. There's no need to be here. There's nothing happening here. I'm leaving."

Not only does my friend come outside, but our accomplice came outside too. I thought, what the hell are you doing?

While I'm headed toward the car, I realize someone lost the keys to our getaway car. Once I realized the keys were lost, I ran as fast as I could to another neighborhood. My friend got caught that night, our accomplice who was on the inside went back to get his phone and he went to jail. I was home free for the time being, but I really didn't know what to do, so I just started traveling around the state. I was on the run between Greensboro, Fayetteville, and sometimes Atlanta sleeping on folks' couches. I was trying not to think about what happened and kept thinking about how I got away.

I tried to go about my life as normal as possible, however my life at that time was anything but normal—until *that day*. I remember it like it was yesterday. I had been out for a while and hadn't been arrested like my friend. I didn't know I was a prime suspect. I'm thinking everything was cool and I would support my friend who got caught the best way I could and that would be that.

The crime took place April 22, 2010. About a couple weeks later, I told my mom what happened. It was one of the hardest things I ever told her. At first I wasn't going to mention it, but I felt I was really going crazy. I don't know why, but I felt like folks were out to get me, and my mind was sensing something. I felt like everything was a setup. Some might say it was my conscious kicking in or whatever, but I felt I didn't know where else to go. When I told my mom what happened of course she cried. She couldn't believe I did something like that.

On June 24, 2010, I went home like a normal day, ate dinner and went to sleep. I woke up the following morning to a strange knock on the door. My mom came in and said, "It's the police." I knew about police killing people like it's nothing, so I threw my remote control all the way over across the room, and I said, "Well, let me get these last few minutes of sleep."

I don't know how many police officers came in. They had guns pointed at me, and the only thing I hear them say is, "Hands! Hands! Let me see your hands!" I knew right then I was officially going to get arrested for this crime.

Later, it was shared with me that several people told police I was involved with the home invasion. A little bit of evidence pointed in my direction and that was pretty much it.

*　*　*

You don't really know how much time goes by in an interrogation room, or a holding cell, but it goes by pretty quickly. It feels like you're in a time machine. I got arrested early that morning, and I didn't get out until it was dark outside. I didn't even think I was going to get out. I prepared to take whatever came with the situation, but my mom and a few of her friends were able to bail me out.

It was very wild. I was about to deal with the system. I knew quite a few people who had been in this kind of situation. You read about these moments, see them on TV, but it's a totally different experience once you're inside and going through it yourself.

I went on the hunt for a lawyer, which was another daunting process because, again, we didn't have any money. Like *no* money. We searched as far and as wide as we could. Seemed like everybody was telling me, "Yeah, you're going to go down. You're going to jail." It seemed like everybody agreed I should go to jail. Like the whole thing was orchestrated. It got to the point where I was convinced, shit, ok. Guess I'll just go to prison.

Orca Moment: Sometimes the words of other people□especially those in a position to help you□can make you think the worst about yourself and situation. It's very important to have people in your corner who care about what goes in your mind. Whether I was going to jail or not no one, aside from my mom and friends, instilled in me to keep a positive mindset and fight for my life. I learned from that experience just how important it was for me to have control over my own mind. If I didn't, others would gladly control it for me.

I got arrested June 25, 2010, and went through several court dates. People shared with me what to expect, but I really don't remember all that took place. All I could think about was every single wrong decision I ever made that led me to that point. I thought not only about the wrong decisions, I thought about *every* decision.

It's like I snapped out of something. I realized I really fucked up. I *really fucked up*. This was one of the most humbling moments in my life. It got to the point where all I could think about was getting it over with. Getting to the other side of all this and never looking back.

The day finally arrived when I got an email from my attorney saying we had a court date set up for January 18, 2011. I should have known something was up because she said to me, "You made it through Thanksgiving, Christmas, and the New Year." The wording sounded like she was about to tell these folks to send me to jail.

It was hard knowing these would be the last times I would see my family for a little while. I didn't tell my family about what was going to happen except Aunt Tanji and my cousin Courtney. I didn't sleep well, and I can't recall having a good dream at all during that time. Something is taken away from you when you do this type of thing. That's just what happens.

At my court date I don't even remember the judge's name. A few people were there, my mom, her pastor and one of her best friends came to support me. It's important that the court sees you have somebody to support you. I'm sure more would've come if I had told them. They talked about how my mom was involved in the church and how I was doing all these things after getting arrested and before the court date. I was volunteering, working with children, really trying to clean my act up so to speak.

But it was as if the judge just wanted to get rid of me. He acknowledged he was very happy with how I tried to change my life, but then he goes off and says, well they committed a home invasion, and that's just something we don't really tolerate here.

I said to myself, "WTF."

He sentenced me to one count of twenty to thirty-three months for second-degree kidnapping and another count of twenty to thirty-three months for conspiracy of robbery with a dangerous weapon. The sentences were to be served consecutively.

Hearing that, I thought, OK cool. They put me in handcuffs, took me down to the bullpen. I thought, OK, I got a year and eight months, I thought. It's nothing. I'll be alright. I can do that. Then my attorney came down and asked me how I felt.

"You know, this is nothing but a year and a few months," I said. "I can do that."

She looked at me hard.

"No Justin," she said. "That would be if your sentence ran concurrently. Your sentence is running consecutively, so that means you got to do forty to sixty-six months."

When you hear people say things in court you really don't understand. Again, I thought, OK cool, forty months. It wasn't until I did the math on my hand that I realized, yo, *that's three years minimum.*

I looked back at my attorney.

"So you mean I got to be here for three years?" I said. "You can get out my face now."

I was shocked. This was the first time I had to really sit and face this major disappointment. I was twenty-one years old and I had to be locked up for three years. Then my mom comes down. She gave me the most disappointed look I'd ever seen on her face. I'd never before□and never since□seen my mom so hurt. That experience definitely hurt me more than the prison sentence.

"Justin," she said. "What are you going to do?"

I was so zoned out of my damn mind.

"I'm about to go in here and grow some dreads," I said. "I'll see you in 2014."

That's exactly how it went.

County Jail

This was my second time going to jail, however, this time it was definitely different. I knew I would not be leaving for a while. Walking to the pod at the county jail, I see a lot of damn people. Most of them I don't know.

There was a good mixture of people. The majority were black and some Mexicans. I don't remember if I saw a white person. County jail has to be some of the hardest times on an individual. We spent most of the time in our cells. I don't even remember how much time. We ate some of the worst food known to human existence. They even had a plate nicknamed dog food.

I spent my first stint in county jail just shocked at actually being in jail. It wasn't a rough experience, however I wasn't well prepared, especially financially or with my hygiene. A few dudes belonged to gangs. If you weren't in the gang, you might not of had much going on. Some of the guys would fight, rap or try to play basketball.

County jail was my introduction to what prison would be. One thing I noticed was that I didn't have food. There were folks in there eating food that wasn't what the county provided. Dudes also had hygiene or cosmetics products. All I had was the county-issued soap which was like hotel soap. I didn't have deodorant for a long time.

I didn't know about getting money put in your account or all that other good old gravy stuff. I didn't know what to expect. I remember when my mom first sent me some money. I was so happy because it meant I could buy me a little something when the canteen lady came by.

People also asked a lot of questions like where I was from, what happened, or what did I do to get locked up. Most of the guys would say to me, "Man you're bout to go to prison. Man, like, you shouldn't get comfortable with this." I would tell them, I have no choice, I'm just here for the ride. I was already in the mindset of this just being a stepping stone to the next level of my life. One big-ass stepping stone, but a step nonetheless.

* * *

After a while, I started noticing the mentality of different sheriff's deputies. Some of them were cool, some were assholes, however, this one was a real nice woman. Every night when we were in our cells she sang over the speaker. It was like a lullaby, almost. She would just sing us to sleep. I don't know who she was, but it was as if she felt it was her duty to the world to try and make the pod a safer place. It got us to calm down, and that was like one of the most touching things I saw inside county.

When I saw people get bailed out or complete their time I'd think, damn I'm not going to have that experience for a while. I had three years left and I was saying this during my first week. Watching them gave me something to look forward to. They looked so happy, but who knows what they were going back home too, or if it was anything better than this.

While I was in jail, I was surprised by how many letters I wrote. I didn't have a girlfriend, so it was really rough. I felt like I was really going to be doing this on my own, but the truth was I wasn't alone.

Most people were there just doing time. They were what we like to say, *letting the time do them.* They were existing, not doing anything constructive to better themselves. It felt like just a bunch of young guys who were at a camp or something and just couldn't go home. That was an eye-opener to me. It was very different from what I perceived jail to be. Sometimes people came home from jail incredibly smart.

I started to think about what kind of purpose I could have in jail. From the jail canteen, I ordered snacks, soap, deodorant and other stuff. Surprisingly, I received all these goodies the last day before I got shipped to prison. That same day they told me I had to leave it all behind because it was county property. I thought it was some bullshit, but the morning I left I put my purchases by the doors of the folks who looked out for me. Then got ready to head off to prison.

The very first prison I got to was Polk Youth Correctional Facility.

II

Mindset

In this section, you'll see how I continued to grow to become an apex person. You'll see the importance of learning by experience and learning how to work as a unit rather than an individual. You'll walk away understanding the value of knowing yourself and the importance of determination, dedication and discipline. These are core competencies that any individual needs to succeed in life. More importantly, you will see no matter how dark your situation is, you have to create the life you want in your mind first. Only then can you take steps, moment by moment, to get there. It's a marathon, not a race.

Polk Youth Center

The trip to Polk was one of the most eye-opening experiences. I remember hearing a song by Drake and Nicki Minaj on the transport bus called "Moment 4 Life." It was strange, because I thought I was finally getting my journey started. In a way, it was a moment of relief, because I could actually start to get this shit over with.

On the way to Polk, I kept thinking about my homeboy, Chris Houston who we used to call Fat. Before going to prison, all he said was, "They gonna make you fight. You gonna have to fight at Polk, Justin."

On the bus, that was the only thing in my head. People used to call Polk the Polk Gladiator School. Everyone said you had to get involved with your hands at Polk, and nobody was going to save you.

Hell, that's just what it's going to be, I thought. I'm not about to be sitting here going to prison and can't defend myself, or have a crazy rep for being afraid to fight in the penitentiary. I was prepared to accept responsibility for my actions, even if it meant defending my life.

When I got to Polk, the strangest thing in the world happened. It had to be the most humiliating experience in my life. We get off the transport bus, and the first thing we do is take off all our clothes, line up in a straight line with our hands out and cough. The room was full of nothing but men. You start on one side, then you walk to the other side. You get your uniform, or jumpsuit, or onesie, whatever the hell you wanted to call it. Then, you grab your mattress.

Polk is like a big college campus. You still had dorms, but instead of the traditional college campus setting, you get the college "look" with a bunch of dead energy. There was a wall and a fortress on the outside☐in the middle of nowhere.

As I walk across the yard holding all my stuff people ask me where I'm from. I remembered people in county jail saying Polk had a lot of dudes from Charlotte.

"You're going to be aight," they said. "Your homeboys are gonna be there with you."

You see, Polk is a big gang prison. All these guys are in gangs. So walking across the prison yard, that was one of the first questions I get.

"Ayo, what's up my nigga. Ayo, you bang?" he asked.

"Nah," I said.

"Ayo, where you from?"

"I'm from Charlotte."

"Ah shit, another Charlotte nigga, man. Fuck."

That really made me feel a little bit better. I thought, I guess what they were saying is correct. Charlotte niggas on the prison yard, huh?

I walk to the dorm which is one big building. Once I get in, I walk toward the pod. I think, all right, here it is, this is what it's going to be. If I'm going to have to fight, they're gonna have to fight me right here, right now today.

Next, I pull some of the craziest shit in my life. I put my mattress down, I put down all my bags and I did my best to look at every single person in their face when I walked in there. I scan the room from right to left, doing something like a heat check. I did it all again. I looked at everybody. Then the thought came to my head, this shit really ain't what they said it was.

I went to sit at my bunk and put my stuff together. Another guy comes up again with the million-dollar question.

"Yo, where you from man? You bang my nigga?"

"Nah, I don't bang," I say. "I'm from Charlotte."

Luckily, like four dudes in my pod were from Charlotte. They pretty much had everything on lock. It was kind of surreal to see it. It was almost like a movie.

I started to recognize who was the top person in the block, who was there just for some reckless shit, and who was really in the streets, but probably didn't have too much intelligence. Some were what you'd call a boss and some who were just chilling, not really even thinking about making friends or enemies.

There was this one dude who went by the name Selmo. He had a resounding voice in the block and in the pod. Come to find out, he was a high-level member of the Charlotte Kings, which is a gang out of Charlotte. He had some rank, and if you have rank in a street gang coming into prison—especially Polk—you were given a certain level of respect.

One day he came up to me.

"What's up with ya, homeboy? You got something to eat? You good on hygiene?"

"Hell nah, I don't have anything to eat," I said. "Got some food?"

That was the moment I realized it was true when people would say, "you got a lot of homeboys in prison," and I wouldn't have much to worry about. One thing I noticed in prison—that I didn't see much in the free world—was that people showed empathy for your situation and would try to help the best way they could. It was very eye-opening.

Another thing I learned was some people had a different aura about themselves. They walked with a different level of confidence. They had a different energy. We were all there for crime, but this kind of person was more of an apex predator, more of an alpha. There's a reason why someone is the top dog of a pod.

Me and Selmo were pretty cool. We walked the yard and talked daily. He was very interested in knowing what was going on in Charlotte. He also asked me how I got caught up in my crime and situation. After I told him, his answer sounded the same as the others.

"Boy you seem too smart to be in here," he said. "You don't seem soft. I don't know, but something is telling me, like, you're not really supposed to be here, but you did something to get here."

I went further into what led me to prison. I told him not just about the crime, but all the events that led up to it as far back as my senior year in high school. Overall, what I noticed about Selmo was the fact that he wasn't loud and rambunctious like everyone else. I believe by the time he was twenty years old he might have been locked up for five years. So from the age of fifteen, all he had known was the penitentiary. Being imprisoned that young, that long, I hate to say this, but you develop a different level of wisdom and a level of charisma that's different from everyone else.

So even though my stay at Polk wasn't long, I learned a lot when it came to how to carry yourself. You still want to carry yourself with a certain level of respect. You want to be respected, by the guards, by all the other people you're locked up with.

Orca Moment: *Always carry yourself as someone to be respected. I'm not saying to act as if you're better, but understand it's all about respect in prison. Whatever you say you can do, do it. It's not just about being goofy and loud the whole time.*

* * *

At one point during my time at Polk, one dude asked me a question about how much time I had. People talked about this a lot and you never knew if they were lying or not.

"I got three years," I said.

"Oh shit, you said thirty?!"

"Hell no."

"Oh, I thought you said thirty," he said. "Shit, I got thirty."

"Goddamn," I said.

I don't know if he was telling the truth or not.

At Polk, it was a big thing to have someone 'pay rent' especially if you were a scared white boy. Them boys "gonna make you click that card," people would say, which means, whenever *your* folks send *you* money, they send *us* money. Basically, when *you* eat, *we* eat. Simple as that.

I saw a few individuals run up to a white boy. I don't know how they got this in, but someone had an electric screwdriver.

"Look here motherfucker," he said. "You got three options: One, you click that fucking card. Two fight me. Or three, you get stabbed."

The white boy came up with his own option. He hopped up off that fucking bed so quick and ran down to the goddamn door. He told the COs, "Get me the fuck out of here!" He was never allowed back in that pod.

That's what they call a "check off." It was some of the most eye-opening prison shit to me. They didn't stab the man, but it was pretty damn close. Also at Polk, you just get to meet a whole lot of different people. I noticed there were a lot of other gang members or street guys. They all had different positions and they all hung together. They all seem to be kind of cool with me, but I still stuck to myself.

One of the strangest things about this experience was that I actually saw who had intelligence and who didn't. In jail, people's basic needs were met daily. They had food, water, shelter and a place to sleep, but our needs were met in a very dangerous, terrible place—jail.

I met folks from all over the state from Charlotte to Greensboro. They were young dudes, some doing so much time they weren't going to get out until they were gray in the face. Polk youth center was just a big-ass boarding school. You had a lot of people who didn't know much about life and who would never really live life. All they knew were the streets. Some probably knew a little bit more, but in reality, they were too young to know anything about life. You could really tell they wanted more. The majority of everyone didn't want to be there. They called this shit, "truly failing," and I can't blame them. Hell, I was in the same boat.

I didn't stay at Polk long. You see, in prison you're not considered an adult at age twenty-one, so you can't automatically go to the adult prison. You go to Polk Youth Center first to get processed and all that jazz, and then you get shipped out. My time at Polk might have only been two weeks—just enough time to give a taste of what prison is like, but it was about to change because next I was being sent to the adult prison.

Craggy

Leaving Polk to head to Craggy Correctional Center was a whole other level of experience. I woke up early in the morning and the correctional officer told me I was leaving, and yeah, that was that. When I was getting ready to go to the adult facility, I started thinking, damn, what's this part of life going to be like? This is all new.

I told myself I would be able to determine everything about a prison the moment I got there. I was like, you know, just be who you are and stay focused, because this was a big deal. I'm headed to the adult prison.

I had so many stories swirling in my head, and I'd hadn't really been in prison, but like a month and some change. I didn't know what to expect. One thing I did know was, I was going to have to go in there, take off my clothes, squat and cough. It's a terrible process of making sure you don't bring any contraband from one prison to the next.

I don't even remember this trip in detail. When I left, it was the middle of night, so I slept. On the way to Craggy, I was just thinking about where I was going, Asheville, North Carolina and how everything would be new.

When I get there, I notice it's a different prison entirely. It's a little bit smaller. Three buildings, four blocks, cafeteria, basketball court, a humongous yard and that was it. It was a real country mountain prison. All the guards with rank—your captain, lieutenants, superintendent—are all white. That was the other interesting component about prison: You got to see just what this other side of the system really looked like.

My first night at Craggy, I didn't like any part of it. This prison was definitely not to my liking, but I figured I'd try to make the most of it. At Craggy, they were very big on working the road squad or doing some type of work. The very first job I remember having was working on the road squad, picking up trash on the side of a damn mountain. A gunman was in the front, a gunman was in the back and we ate these disgusting peanut butter and jelly sandwiches with milk. I don't know who the hell made up this combination of food. We had a little small cup of water. You had to urinate on the bus. I don't even know if you could piss outside. I remember walking eight hours a day picking up trash on the side of fucking mountain thinking, goddamn, this seems like slavery. Why the fuck are we doing this? Exploitation in prison is real.

At Craggy, I didn't really meet too many people, but I met another Charlotte person, this one dude who I actually went to school with. His name was Man. Me and Man were around the same age. I think Man had been locked up like three more years than I had, so he was like twenty-one years old.

The first thing Man told me was his advice.

"Ay bro, take prison serious, man," he said. "Don't be in here playing, goofing off like the rest of these niggas you going to see, you know. Really take this serious, bruh. Take this as a learning lesson and you going to be good. I promise you. *You going to be good.*"

I was like, all right cool. You know it was always distinct words of wisdom that came from certain people in prison, because we were all in this thing together—especially young dudes. We were the youngest dudes. Probably the youngest dudes in the adult spread around the entire state of North Carolina.

One day I ran across another dude who we called Blacc. I can tell Blacc is from Charlotte just by how he carried himself, like a typical Charlotte person. He was a very cool, very chill type of individual. It always amazes me how prison has such a humbling effect on people. Like most people, Blacc had been locked up a while. I think he had done like four years, and he might have only been like twenty-two years old. Blacc told me all about all the ins and outs of prison. We were both the same age, and a lot of things we talked about were about girls.

One day I had a very interesting conversation with Blacc. It was February 18, as matter of fact, and I had just gotten my last haircut and was about to grow my dreadlocks for the rest of the bid. I don't know how this conversation came about, but it's not like this is the first time we had a real conversation.

"Man, today is the day one of my homeboys got killed in 2007," I said.

"Was it on the eastside?" he asked.

"Yeah."

"Was it in Stonehaven Apartments?" he asked.

"Yeah."

He paused.

"I knew you looked real familiar, bruh," Blacc says. "I was there at that party that night."

Then there was this one awkward moment, where I know the look in my eye changed towards him. I felt my energy change. It was almost like time just stood still because Travis's killer was never caught. I'm looking at him like, who the hell are you for real?

"Nah, bruh, I ain't have nothing to do with it, bruh," he said quickly. "I just lived over there, but I ain't have nothing to do with it. But you know, like, it was just, you know, how people were just talking in the hood when they were just talking about it. It was a real messed up situation."

I believed him. Some strange part of me believed him. I had learned over the years to trust my instincts. Another part of me was thinking, Why would you lie? I mean, you could have a reason to lie, but I didn't really think he did. If he did lie, he damn sure played the hell out of me.

Within that conversation, we ended up becoming cool and tight. Again, you develop these relationships, these types of bonds in prison with people. Like I said before, Craggy wasn't to my liking. I understand, there's no prison to anyone's liking but, at Craggy I was just like, yo, get me the hell out of here. I'm not really feeling this prison.

I remember distinctly how I got into it with a lieutenant. He wore a white shirt and had some bars on his shirt. I got into it with him about something, and he sent me to the hole for a few hours. I'm in prison less than a month and I already got sent to the hole. I don't really remember for what. I just remember that within the next few days after I got out, they said:

"Hey, pack your bags. It's time for you to go to a new prison."

"And where will that be?" I asked.

"Mountain View."

Mountain View CI

ow, Mountain View Correctional Institution was a very, very, very different experience. It got the name Mountain View because that's what you have—a view of the mountain. The prison itself sits at the top of a mountain surrounded by mountains with nowhere to go. A trend I started noticing with prisons is they put you in these locations where it's really, really hard for you to escape.

On the way there people were saying, "You know, at Mountain View it's the good old boy system." I didn't know what the hell that meant. During my transfer, I didn't have to go to the transit center they call Sandy Ridge, which is a big field out by Greensboro, NC where you get off one bus and head to another. It was a straight-up drop off to Mountain View.

When we arrived at Mountain View, we hopped out of the bus. I remember this CO, his name was Grindstaff. The first thing he said to me was, "If a man acts like a man, I treat him like a man. If it's anything else, then I'll treat you by how you act." I thought, that's pretty straightforward or whatever, but this was a very peculiar camp. It was all white and I mean *all white*. When I head to my block, the Mountain View facility is like what you see on prison shows. It's very spacious with three floors of prison cells in a U-shaped fashion. You have two TVs in the block, twenty-two rooms. On the first two floors, you have a bunkmate, and if you stay on the third floor, you are able to have your own cell and don't share a room with anybody. It was a very big clean indoor facility. You didn't really have to touch outside if you didn't want to.

I saw over one hundred and ten people out on my first big day in the block. It was a mixture of younger guys and older guys who seemed very relaxed for the most part. There were a lot of white inmates too. Black people were outnumbered, but not by much.

I got introduced to people who asked where I was from. When I told folks I was from Charlotte, I instantly started running across other people from Charlotte on this block. I ran across a man they called Rabbit. Rabbit was the boss of all bosses in the prison system at Mountain View. Rabbit was the canteen man. He was the hustle man. He was really about nothing but business in prison, no ifs ands or buts about it. When he asked where I was from, I told him I lived on Beatties Ford Road.

"Yeah, I'm the old Earle Village," he said.

"Old Earle Village?"

"Yeah, you know, before they knocked it down in the '90s, the real Uptown project. That's where I grew up."

After the conversation with Rabbit, I went to my bed and sat down in my bunk. I had a roommate named Ty, who was Asian. Funny thing about Ty was he had lived in Charlotte. I think Ty was thirty-three years old and had been locked up for seven years. He would tell me how he was about to go home. He was a real cool guy. He was very knowledgeable about sports gambling.

Sports gambling was major in prison, especially at Mountain View where you didn't have a lot of drugs. Security is so packed you didn't have a lot of things there, so gambling was very big. What made it interesting was that gambling circles were ran almost like they were on the outside world. A lot of the white guys held down the gambling. It was almost unreal. It was almost the opposite of what I had known about prison in my short time.

During the first few days of my stay, I was walking to the chow hall and I saw somebody I knew. Someone by the name of Peway. I was like, wow, damn, OK. I know him.

"Yo, what's up man," he said. "How you doing? You good?"

I knew Peway for some years before from playing basketball in Charlotte. He was a good dude who just got into some situations that led him to where he was at, but at the end of the day he was still a genuine dude.

Another day, I'm sitting in the block watching the game and another homeboy of mine named Tyrone comes in the block and says, "Yo, who's Justin?"

I still don't have a prison name so I say, "I'm Justin."

"Yo, Petway, the boy who look like Anthony Davis, wants you outside," Tyrone says.

So I go out there and meet with Petway. It's real refreshing to see someone you knew from your childhood whether it be in prison or not. We talked about life, how we got caught up in crime, and all of our similar situations.

Petway was someone that I ended up growing cool with. Also, he could play real good basketball. He told me that Mountain View is a pretty cool camp, and he was on his way home. He was on the down side of his bid, meaning that the bulk of his time was over. Even though my time was just getting started, he told me the same as everyone else: "The time will fly by, bro. Just keep your head up and everything will work out."

A few weeks, maybe a month or two pass, (who really remembers). I remember everything I learned from Polk and Craggy about how to conduct and carry yourself, because people were watching you at all times, not just the guards, but other inmates as well. It was around this time, I really started noticing just how much power and charisma, my man Rabbit had. Remember earlier in the book when I said me and my college friends would watch documentaries of old school hustlers from the '80s and early '90s? Well, Rabbit was one of them.

At one point, I was very low on money. I thought to myself, damn if you hollered at the canteen man, he'll help you out. He'll look out for you. So I decided to hit him up.

"Yo, Rabbit," I said. "I need some food and some soup and what not. I'm going to be straight up with you, I don't know when my mom or family can send me some money, but I'm gonna keep you up to date on it. When I have it, then I'll definitely bring it to you. Whatever works for you. If it's bit by bit or all at once. I'm gonna do what I say I'm gonna do and pay you."

"Aite, man. Don't worry about it," Rabbit said. "That's cool, man, just don't worry about it."

Rabbit let me hold some soaps, some canteens and what not, and that was that.

> ***Orca Moment:*** *The only thing you have in prison—not just in prison, but life—is your word. You have to put your life on your word. Crazy thing is that people in prison understand this better than people who never went. Especially those of you in business, if you wish to succeed in life, put a high value on your word.*

So, after Rabbit and I talked about my situation, he asked the same thing everyone else did who was in a "position of power" within the block: "What the hell you doing here? How'd you end up in this situation?"

As usual I explained my circumstances up to that point. People often could relate to me, how I tried to change my situation, especially when it came to finances. I started noticing a lot of people in jail or prison ended up there mainly because of financial disparities.

*** *** ***

My first few months in prison I tried to sleep the time away. I slept all damn day. People would say, "Bro you can't sleep that time away," and I replied, "Well, shit let me try." My whole goal was to get this day over with and get the next one started. I didn't care how many hours I slept. Until one morning.

At Mountain View, there was something called count time, it's probably the most annoying thing in the damn world ever in prison. I didn't know anybody who liked count time because that means you got to wake your ass up from a good night's sleep, identify yourself and make sure you're alive. You're moving. All you got to do is move to prove you didn't escape in the middle of the night. As if there was anywhere to go from Mountain View anyway. It was almost a fortress how they had it set up. Hell, you could escape and go deal with bears, mountain lions and the mountain if you wanted to. If you did, you'd probably realize you might be better off just doing the damn time.

After count time, I'd sleep until I hear a lot of noise in the block, maybe around 12 p.m. or whatever, but on this one particular day I got a knock on my door. It was Rabbit.

"Aite, bruh, you said your mama can't send no money, right?" he asked.

"Yea," I said.

"Then get your mother-fucking ass up, and hit this yard and learn how to hustle out here, man."

I paused and looked at him like, what the fuck?

"Aite," I replied.

That started my career as a penitentiary hustler.

All The Way In

I n 2011, Rabbit and I would hit the yard hard *daily*. From the very beginning, Rabbit gave me some advice.

"Listen, they're many hustles you can have out here," he said. "You can't run the canteen, because that's mine that I took when I first got here. You can play on the card table, you can loan stamps, sell tobacco, etc. However, you can't hustle like how we used to do back in the day when I was your age."

Rabbit was in his early forties at the time.

"Nowadays, you have to actually have an immaculate talk game with these people because most of the folks in the yard at this camp are white," he said. "The prison is run by white people, and they do their best to protect them. It wasn't like back in the '90s when it was every man for themselves. The game is very different now."

First thing we did was go around to meet folks.

"You got to realize who got all the money," Rabbit said. "It ain't your homeboys. Most of these niggas were broke on the street, and it didn't change once they came to prison, so don't fall for the bullshit. Some of the guys in the block who had all the money and their family was taking care of them on a tremendous level were probably homosexual or had a crime that wasn't a 'black crime'"

He went on to say that it's all about how you have a product. You get

71

whatever they desire and you sell it. Once you have what they have, you got to continuously mold that relationship. I didn't know at the time, but Rabbit was not only showing me how to do business with other races on the prison yard, but he was teaching me the real world of business in general.

My first introduction to entrepreneurship was in prison. I started running a canteen business with Rabbit. In prison, you can only have up to twenty-five items from the canteen in your locker. If you exceed that amount, the COs will try to label you as running a canteen in the block. One of the first things Rabbit said was to "use your locker for some of the canteen items, and if somebody tries to borrow some food, if I ain't got it, I know you got it. We can go on from there."

That's what we did for a while. What I mean by a while was like several months. I even learned how to keep an inventory. One of the most valuable skills I got out of all of this was learning how to make an invoice. Every Sunday night I would put together what people owed me from the previous week. I would do this on Sunday because mail wouldn't run on the weekends. That meant people didn't receive any money until Monday.

I remember one time writing an invoice for someone that was upwards of fifty dollars. What was crazy about that was we could only spend forty dollars per week from the canteen. The guy had his family send me twenty-five dollars, and he purchased the other twenty-five dollars piece by piece to settle his bill. Running the store was very beneficial, because during periods when my family didn't send me any money I was not hurting or starving in the block.

Orca Moment: Ask yourself, how do you stand out? How do you make yourself the top one percent of the one percent? Everyone, the entire yard respected Rabbit. Everybody said the same thing, "He's always about his business." The lesson you must take from this moment is consistency. How you carry yourself needs to be consistent. What you stand for, the energy you bring, and how you treat people needs to be consistent. Conscious day-to-day-consistency. If you're in business, your message needs to always be consistent so no one can ever second guess who you are and what you stand for.

Another thing Rabbit showed me was the gambling side of prison. Rabbit ran a game called pick of the week. We would come up with these tickets which were no more than strips of paper. For example, the paper was recycled signature paper. When you sign for something, you have the white side, under that you have a yellow paper and a green paper under that. We would get these sheets of paper and write down the teams playing for the 1 p.m. football games. Then, we'd take a razor and just cut them all the way down the side and those were the tickets. All week starting Monday or Tuesday we would hit the yard and pass out tickets. Then sometimes, if you couldn't get a ticket, people would just write down teams on a sheet of paper.

We would do this every week, Rabbit, myself, and another dude from Charlotte named Hustle. Rabbit had a whole system on the yard. Not only did Rabbit have a good way with the other inmates, but the COs as well. It's like he was hustling right in front of them under their nose. We had to be real discreet about how we did this. Mountain View wasn't going for any of the bullshit. If they saw you do something, they would write you up in a heartbeat.

He knew how to talk to him, not in a submissive way, but in a way that gained respect better than anyone else. He would tell me about all the guards, who was really an asshole, who was alright, who was young, who was hip.

Then one day Rabbit talked to me about religion.

"Man, if you don't really feel good with Christianity, no more," he said. "You should explore other options of discipline, because in here you're going to need it."

That's when he introduced me to the Moorish Science Temple of America. This is where my level of understanding and learning rose to a whole other level. I started reading material that I didn't grow up reading. What I respected so much about the teachings was the fact it spoke to the greatness of being black.

So there was a sign we would do when we saw other members of the Moorish Science Temple. You would hold your hand out, five fingers spread out, and place them on your heart. This represents the five highest principles known to man: love, truth, peace, freedom and justice.

One particular day, I greeted someone with the sign. There was this one CO named Officer Taylor who saw us. Officer Taylor was a bit of a prick. You could tell he probably didn't like black people and thought that we were nothing. When he saw us he said:

"Hey are you a Blood? You must be a Blood. I need an STG on you."

STG means you are a part of a security threat group, basically a gang member. I told him I wasn't in a gang. I walked back from the chow hall to the block and he just kept walking behind me saying he was "going to do some counting in F block."

"Do what you got to," I said. "It's not going to change a damn thing of what I told you."

After count time is over, I get called to the sergeant's office. Sergeant Duckett, he was a different type of officer. He respected you as an individual. I'm not going to sit here and say he was your best friend, but he was an old-school corrections officer. He knew what it was like when inmates used to fight COs. He wasn't your friend, but he didn't have to be your enemy as long as you respected him.

Taylor was in the sergeant's office saying something about how he stopped me because I was doing a gang symbol.

"Bruh, I'm not even in a gang," I said. "And y'all know I'm not."

"Well then what are you telling me?" Taylor said. "You telling me I was wrong?"

"Yeah, you're wrong and you a damn lie."

"So, you going tell me how to do my job?"

"If that's how it looks, like it has to go, then it is what it is."

That moment was the first time I wanted to ever really fight a CO. I looked at him dead in his eye as he looked at me. I'm telling you Sergeant Duckett is old school, and I really believe he would have let it go down, but he noticed that I was not going to be disrespected, so the sergeant broke it up. I'm not saying being in a gang is disrespectful, but I wasn't in one, and I never in my life claimed to be in one.

After that, I think I reached a new level of prison status. Folks told me they heard what happened. It was loud as hell, and I just wasn't about to back down. I actually wanted it to happen. In my eyes I had nowhere to go. Period. So I thought, let's make the best of this moment.

After that incident blew over, I started really admiring what I was learning about myself. See Rabbit wasn't only introducing me to the prison game of hustling. He was also introducing me to the game of overall personal development, and teaching me how to be better than I was when I came into prison. Sometimes, I see Rabbit as my very first business coach of sorts. He would always say, "Handle your business first. It might take five to ten minutes, an hour or hours. No matter what, take care of it first, once you're done, you can then play the rest of the day." He would share these little jewels of wisdom with me. He was a real shot caller, always witty, never letting nobody play. He didn't even have to get loud. He just knew how to talk to people in ways to make them understand, "This is what it is. This is what we gonna do. Let's make it work."

Another thing Rabbit liked about me was that I could play basketball. Now Mountain View was very different than all the other two camps that I played on at Polk and Craggy. I really didn't have enough time to play basketball. The first time I played basketball at Mountain View I wore these little low top Chuck Taylors. They were the shoes the state would give you when you came to prison, and they were terrible. Guys in the yard would say, "You go get you some shoes, bruh. You'll get hurt in those. You going to have to get you some New Balance shoes, if you want to play basketball."

"Alright, I'll get some," I said.

When I put in my order for shoes, it probably took about two weeks to get there. Once they arrived, it was really on and popping. I was supremely out of shape, but we played every day. You always hear these rumors that there's a lot of good talent hooping in prison. I started noticing just how much basketball talent was on the court in prison.

On our side of the prison, we had this one dude named BuShawn, we had this dude who went by And One, we had me, we had a lot of folks who played basketball, and sometimes games would almost be like collegiate level.

Everybody would be out there. I mean *everybody*.

Basketball in prison is where I learned a different type of mental game. Sometimes, it didn't matter how good you were or how big you were. Most everybody in prison is in some type of shape, and if you are in shape, you can be a force.

One of the best people I ever played in prison was BuShawn. He had to be like 6'6", from New York. He had a scholarship to St. John's University, but whatever crime he did, it got him some time. Of course, he wasn't able to take advantage of the scholarship, but he was very good on the court. My first year and a half I was never able to beat him. It was undeniable he was the best player on the yard. It was just one of those situations where you had to raise your level of play. It left me questioning how I would ever get on a level to beat this dude.

I remember one game specifically I had BuShawn down in the game. We were playing to sixteen points and the score was ten to five. I thought, "I finally got this man. I'm finally going to beat him." Next thing you know this man pulls off some Michael Jordan shit. He starts breaking down the defense, driving at will, making all the good shots, then ends the game with a banked three-point shot from the hash line, and walks off. I'm like, "What the hell just happened?"

Basketball was just another outlet, until I started training. I had a friend named Ock. The dude was cut up. I told him I didn't want to put on a lot of muscle, but I did want to be cut up.

"Well shit, hit up the pull-up bar with me," he said.

We started off very small doing pull ups here and there. I did probably about two or three a day. Calisthenics was one of the roughest things I ever had to do when it came to exercise, because pulling my own body weight was something I was not used to doing.

"You got to come out here every day," Ock would say. "You got to do them every day, and you'll start seeing different results. It might take a while, but, hell, you got nowhere to go."

Orca Moment: If you train every day and consistently yourself, you are bound to reach different results.

Out on the yard, I had Rabbit showing me how to hustle and introducing me to the Moorish Science Temple. Inside the temple were some other brothers who were just brilliant. These were the guys you'd hear about in movies who read tons of books and did nothing but study. They were kind of like the Malcolm Xs of the time—except they weren't getting out.

We had a grand sheik named Carlos Autry-El and an assistant grand sheik, Flowers-El. They were the type of individuals, some would say, are supremely radical. You might call them woke, but they were conscious beyond belief, and this level of consciousness allowed me to see how serious I needed to take myself. On the street, I was never conscious of myself like that. Mountain View is where I became supremely conscious reading the Moorish Science Temple teachings and reading other types of history of black people. It allowed me to really tap into the brilliance of who I was as a black man.

The Moorish Science Temple is an Islamic type of faith. One of the things you learned was how to carry yourself differently from everyone else. You learned a different level of respect and a higher level of clarity. It was a level of confidence where you know who you are and no one can rock you off of that, no matter how hard they tried, no matter who they were. I would write home to my family about it, and people had opinions or whatever, but being in Moorish Science really is what shifted my mind to know my own level of brilliance.

Those were the first few months of my introduction to prison life. I took some time to get into a groove and adjust to prison. As a matter of fact, it wasn't until my eighth month in prison that I became content—not in a happy way—and just accepted that this is where I'm going to be. I never thought about going home. Of course, I wanted to, but it wasn't like it was in the beginning when I was praying for a release. I really became what they call—I hate to say this—a convict. My days consisted of working out, doing business hustling on the yard, being in my studies and avoiding the repetitive bullshit that comes from being in prison. I was officially all the way in.

Ride The Gas

B y the time summer rolled around we were really doing well playing basketball. Like I said, I was already in a good routine until the most awkward thing happened. One day I was working out and someone said, "Hey F block, y'all trying to play us in some basketball?" It was some guys from G block. Of course, we agreed, and that started a whole tournament during the summer.

We would play for canteen money and it was like our own version of professional basketball. Every single day we were on the yard playing basketball. At first, it just started out with us and G block, then everybody else around the yard wanted in. There were four different blocks on the East Wing at Mountain View, E, F, G, H, and everyone wanted in. This was one of the best ways to pass the time for guys who grew up playing basketball.

The night before all this started, BuShawn transferred to a different prison. Before he left, he said, "Well damn, now the top spot for the best basketball player on the yard is wide open." The competitor in me wanted that spot.

Our block, F block, really had the best, most consistent team. The team was made up of me, my roommate Ty, Ock, Larry, and a few other people. We were really out there hooping every day. That's just how we passed the time, but while I was also consistently playing basketball, I was also becoming consciously aware of who I was.

I remember walking the yard with Rabbit and a few of the other Moors. I would recite one hundred and one quotes from the Prophet Noble Drew Ali. I finally learned how to really study, and used the dictionary to learn words I didn't understand well. The definitions of the words helped me make sense of what I was reading. It opened my mind to new meanings of language. I remember thinking, damn I never had this experience with Christianity was having with the Moorish Science Temple and Prophet Noble Drew Ali. I learned to have a bit of structure and order with my thought process and my life.

One day, I was on the yard playing basketball and I forgot about a Moorish Science Temple meeting. I had to go inside, get my stuff together, and run to one of the Friday meetings. The Grand Sheik at that time, Autry-El said, "See, that's what I'm talking about. He came here with sand and dirt in his eyes. He's committed to be here."

Orca Moment: Regardless if you have ten minutes or five minutes, you show up. You show your dedication. Period. You show up regardless. Eighty percent of success is all about showing up. You aren't guaranteed a "next time" in this life. Always show up when you can.

Throughout my entire time at Mountain View, and prison in general, it was all about staying true to your commitments. You have nowhere to go. All you had in prison was say what you were going to do and doing what you said you would do.

One day Grand Sheik Carlos Autry-El was shipped to a different prison and Level-Bey became the grand sheik. Rabbit moved up to assistant grand sheik, which is someone who heads the temple. It's a role similar to a pastor of a church. Every Friday we would have demonstrations, and it was so profound to me how such a small number of people, no matter what their religion of preference, were taking action to change their life.

I remember the first Friday I did a demonstration in prison. I don't even remember the actual text I referred to, but I was very big on your thought patterns. Your thoughts become your words and your words become your actions. During my time in prison, we were always focusing on what thoughts were going on in our head.

Then during that same summer, I decided to participate in Ramadan for the first time with some of the Muslim brothers at Mountain View. Participating in Ramadan was another great moment that taught me extreme discipline. We could only eat and drink water when the sun was down, around 6 a.m. or 6 p.m. and had to live our life every day as you would normally. So if you worked out hard or played basketball, you had to keep doing that the entire thirty days and read the Holy Quran, too.

On those summer days playing basketball, we could only let water touch our lips—no real drinking. That opened up a different level of mental toughness for me that I didn't know even existed. It's just another reason why I fell in love with mental toughness now and teach such things to my clients.

When it came to the Holy Quran, I didn't know what to read, but my homeboy Ock knew what to do. That was the first time in my life I read an entire religious book. It was very profound. I learned that most of these religions speak the same language. It had me thinking, why do we hate each other? What is the deal? I learned how to become consciously aware of myself. That summer at Mountain View I can say really changed me forever. At times, I even forgot I had time to do in prison.

Orca Moment: The most valuable thing in this world isn't money. It's time and relationships. I fell in love with being the master of my time.

My first year in prison felt like we were playing professional basketball, because again at that time, my mom went awhile without sending me money, and I had to really learn how to make it off the yard my own for some time. I also learned how to be the master of my time. I knew I was onto something great. I started learning about the desire, dedication, process, patience and formula it took to become great at anything. I started noticing the reason people make it to the top is because they're dedicated to the process, not just the accolades that come with it.

As summer 2011 came to a close, Rabbit approached me with a question.

"Hey man, listen," he said. "We got the basketball league coming up this year. I won it last year. I beat the gym team. We're going for it again. Are you trying to play?"

"Hell yeah," I said. "It's not like I have anything else to do."

So now we have the prison basketball league. What's funny is I remember the first time playing, it was like getting ready for a real game. We had these referees who wore black and white shirts and I said to myself, yo, did they give us *real* referees? I walked up to him and I asked, "Ayo, are you a real ref?" He said, "No man, I'm in prison like you." I think, OK, whatever. I was kind of disappointed a bit. I thought we had people come in to referee our basketball games, and to me that would have been so dope.

I remember the first time we played the gym team. They had this guy named DJ, an older dude named Jack, this guy from Charlotte named Smoke, and a few other people. They were a *really* good team. I remember thinking, why the hell are they so good? Hell, they be in the gym all the time. They *work* in the gym. That's all they do, play basketball in the gym, hang out in the gym shooting hoops and doing whatever, which had to be amazing. Who wouldn't want that job in prison?

The first time we played them, I think they beat us pretty good. I didn't think we were going to have a clear-cut victory or an easy win, however, at that moment I knew that this was about to be serious. I was like, all right, so we got some competition now. Most of the prison league was pretty competitive. We had the second-best team, according to the record in the league. On our team we had Ock, Ty (from Statesville), KD, Black, myself and this one dude named James from Greensboro, who happened to be very young with *a lot* of time. People would just talk about how much time he had to do at such a young age.

I thought, well damn how much time are we talking about? So I decided one day to just straight up ask him. One thing I couldn't stand ever since I was a child, was being caught up in a rumor mill. I always felt it's just best to ask what's on your mind. Plus me and James were pretty cool since we were both pretty young.

One day I walked up to him and asked:

"What's up, James. Niggas on the yard talking and saying you got a lot of time to do. Personally, I'd rather just know from you than hear other people talk. So how much time do you have left?"

"I got thirty-three more years until I can go home, Slim."

I know my face, said *what?!*

"Hell yea," James said. "I'm going to be here for a little minute my boy."

Sometimes you get so used to being in prison, that you forget like damn we still in prison. It is mind-boggling he had that much time left.

During this basketball league, we are still going about our day-to-day lives. I remember getting a visit from my mom. She drove all the way to Mountain View to see me. The visit with my mom was so cool. I just really loved the small moments we had together. Then again, I never really knew I was going on in my mom's head. I just hope that she didn't think she failed as a parent.

My mom did all she could, and I loved her for it. She would usually bring my Aunt Henrietta, who was the best friend of one of my childhood friends.

I remember I had a pen pal, too. For the sake of respect, I'm not going to use her real name, but she would always write me. Writing her was probably one of the best things going on for me at that time. She even sent me money. I remember going to visitation looking forward to a kiss and the smell of a woman, a black woman at that. There were no black women that worked at Mountain View, so outside of visitation, I didn't see any black women for a long time.

That was my life back then. That year, basketball was really something to help take my mind off being in prison. The only thing I had to look forward to were visits, basketball, Moorish Science Temple meetings and the occasional sports that came on TV, but that was all I needed. I was always tapping deeper into my consciousness asking myself, "How far can I push myself?"

We finished the basketball season with a record of 11-1. I played one of the best all-around basketball games of my life that year. I finished the game with thirty-three points, twelve assists and nine rebounds—one rebound shy of a triple-double.

When the playoffs came around, it was different. Of course, we beat everybody in the playoffs. It came down to us versus the gym team. We had to pick up this one dude out the bus who could really play. His name was Conrad and we said, "We beating these folks today, goddamn it."

So the first playoff game we played against the gym team was a tough game. I don't remember how we won but, I know we won that game. It was one of the first times in my life where my team actually beat the favorites. Growing up, my team would always get close, but never win.

In the playoffs, we played the best two out of three. We won one and had one more to go. After that first game, we laced up against them the same night. The gym usually had two games a night so there was plenty of time to play again.

Again, we were in another tight game with the gym team, and it came down to the last few shots of the game. Somebody on our team had to make free throws, to make it a two-possession ball game. I remember Conrad said some shit like, "Man, I just want y'all boys to know, man, no matter what, I love you all to death." Long story short, we won that game too. I hadn't played basketball in so many years, but I remember most of the time I never beat the best team until then. I felt like I was on top of the world.

We won the championship and that same year I won MVP of the prison basketball league. My 2011 prison experience was almost unreal. It still had its ups and definitely had its downs, but it was a crazy experience nonetheless.

And let's not forget about gambling. Like I mentioned before, gambling was very crazy. Gambling was what most people did in prison. If you didn't gamble, what the hell were you doing with yourself? When you gambled in prison, you were looking to win money. The money is in the form of stamps, and it's a way of getting canteen goods.

I remember in the fall of 2011, my roommate Ty would come in every week and be like, "Yo, Slim. I got Mark's tickets, I got Rabbit's, I got college football, what you trying to do?"

Mark was a guy who ran the big board for gambling on the NFL. I said, "Damnit, let's go ahead and do all of them, but let's really focus on the big pick of the week board run by Mark." Like I said, we were gambling away our time. I was doing it so much I thought I was in Las Vegas. That's all you did in prison. When the yard shut down and sports came on, you would gamble, gamble, gamble, gamble.

I remember on Sunday, specifically, we had survived all the 1 p.m. games. In the NFL you probably got like five or six 1 p.m. games and luckily they only aired Sunday games. Then the 4:25 p.m. games came on. We made it through those games, too, and then it was down to the last game of the night. It was the Philadelphia Eagles versus the New York Giants, and we needed the Eagles to win, otherwise, we would have been in a tie with somebody.

So me and Ty are standing the entire time, biting our nails, watching this game, and I just said, "You know what? I'm gonna stay positive. We gonna win this motherfucka." Next thing you know, it comes down to like the fourth quarter. (I always noticed in gambling it comes down to the fourth quarter.) I'm watching this game and I'm thinking man, it's over. All of a sudden, Eli Manning drops back and this man gets sacked, and I want to say he fumbled the ball, and the Eagles ran it in for the touchdown.

I hollered. I ran upstairs, went to bed and closed my eyes ready for the next day. Ty came in saying he was getting stuff tomorrow and that we would bring it back to the block tomorrow. I had the most stamps, the most snacks and the most canteen ever in my life. We probably had something like four hundred stamps, so that was two hundred stamps each. We had several cosmetic items. That was a big win, however, it didn't end. We were on a roll. I started noticing a trend.

Orca Moment: *You have to notice trends in business and life. Notice when you are just really, really, really winning.*

Not only did we hit that big, I'm pretty sure we hit Rabbit's 1 p.m. pick of the week NFL ticker as well. That got us another two hundred stamps. Now the whole compound knew we were always winning, and we weren't playing around. We were sitting on three hundred stamps apiece. I don't remember calling my mom asking for money. The following week, we won in the college football games as well which was another like three hundred stamps split.

For a long time, it was just winning streak, after winning streak, after winning streak. When you're hot, just like in sports, you ride that wave. When you're hot in life, you ride that wave.

Orca Moment: When you see yourself winning, smash the gas and lean in. Keep going without fear until the wheels fall off, because that's when you will really start seeing gains.

2012

As we got closer to Thanksgiving 2011, I realized this would be my first holiday here. I told myself the holidays really didn't mean much as long as I was in prison. It was just another day that I was ready to get over with, and onto the next one. It was amazing, however, the way the atmosphere and environment changed. People started becoming more friendly, people were sharing more food. The prison was giving out different types of food. You could go back for seconds if you wanted. The whole entire country operates differently during holidays, and prison was no different.

Thanksgiving was cool. It was the time of year when everyone was looking forward to ordering their holiday package. The prison would send around this big holiday form for you to fill out so you could order unique food items that weren't served in the regular canteen store. It was mainly a lot of different sweets and snacks that would probably put you in a diabetic coma if it wasn't for us working out nonstop.

The holidays in prison were just really about eating, watching basketball and football, but my favorite holiday was not Christmas at all. My birthday was cool. A few people got me some gifts, some cards and that was it. My new favorite holiday was New Year's Day. I remember on December 31, watching ABC. The clock struck midnight, and it was January 1, 2012. and I told my homeboy Ock happy New Year, and he said, "Boy, you one step closer to going home, ain't cha?"

"Hell yeah," I said.

I was excited because it gave me hope that I would get out. It was like the guys said in county jail that time flies by on the yard. I was already calculating how much longer I had in prison down to the second. I knew I wouldn't go home until May 12, 2014. It was January 1, 2012. I had two years, four months and eleven days.

2012 brought about some new things. We still did the block versus block basketball games. Some people were shipped out, some people came in, but overall the block was still pretty much the same. I gave more demonstrations at the Moorish Science Temple.

One thing that was just a big shock to me was I had a job cleaning the showers at night. I never knew it and was like, dang I had a job this whole time? That was one thing that kept me in the block, which was key because that's how I was able to keep my business going. The shower job was only paying forty-five cents a day, so if you want to talk about slavery, there you go.

When we started getting new guys—since I had more prison experience—I could tell when someone was just arriving in prison just by seeing how they walked. This one guy comes to the block who's about 6'7" tall. He came from Greensboro but he was from New Orleans. We called him NO, because he was from New Orleans. He was a very intelligent brother who was a member of the Nation of Islam before coming to prison. He told me how he used to play basketball overseas for a few teams, but got caught up in some trouble at home. I didn't really care about any of that. All I thought in my mind was, he can *train* me. I asked if he would and he agreed.

The next morning, we got up and started working out. We would do this religiously day after day. You would've thought I was about to go play for a college or something. As a matter of fact, one of my goals was to play for Johnson C. Smith after going home from prison. A lot of my time in prison was spent training. Training my mind, training my body, training my viewpoint and changing my mindset.

Edward Montrell, who we called NO, was great. Even in prison, I noticed my game elevated. I was able to find different ways of improving myself. Even then I learned that people found ways to condemn what they didn't understand. I would always hear just folks making negative comments like, "You be out there shooting out all day and still be missing." In my head I would respond back saying, damn, why the hell they always talking?

When you are working on improving yourself, other people subconsciously have bad things to say. They don't understand what makes you want to change. Instead, they would say, "You're not going anywhere. You're going to be just like me."

Orca Moment: Drown out the noise. Other individuals who don't want anything outside of prison, who never who never knew what day-to-day improvement looks like—it's no fault of their own. People will tear you down and not even know they're tearing you down because that's how they were brought up.

2012 brought about some magnificent changes. One big change was they ended up moving my homeboy Rabbit out of the block. They moved him to H block. He was making a lot of noise as far as hustling was concerned. A lot of the white inmates didn't like that, because they thought they had total control of the camp.

Rabbit bullied his way into the penitentiary yard and really made a name for himself. He ended up leaving me his canteen hustle in the block. Now this was my first time ever truly having the canteen to myself and it was a different level of responsibility. I couldn't just be regular 'ole Justin or Slim anymore. I had to carry myself totally differently which meant staying the hell out of trouble. I'm not saying I was in a lot of trouble, but I had to stay out of the way entirely.

Whether that was being in the block, outside of working out I had to be available for people, who wanted snacks and canteen. Being the canteen man is a very detailed business, and you had to keep a lot of inventory. You didn't want to take too much shit, but I knew I had to carry myself in a different way if I wanted to stay in business. I'm pretty sure some of the COs knew I was the new canteen man, however I didn't want to give them a reason to just write me up or move me out the block.

To really prosper as canteen man, you had to put people on a little bit of restriction. There were some people who just wanted a lot of snacks and food, and you never knew if they were going to ship out. Rabbit would say, you don't lend out food on certain days because you don't know if they're planning on leaving and leaving you with a big bill. I admit, running the canteen in the beginning was very rough. I didn't really know what I was doing and learned curve every step of the way. Eventually, I got pretty decent, not to the level of Rabbit, but I got pretty decent.

I started knowing which people would pay me back with no problem and started understanding just how to deal with folks who might have money issues. I knew who I could lend to, who not to lend to, and know who to chalk up as a loss.

That year was a big year of learning about entrepreneurship in the prison system, if that even sounds correct. In 2012, I also received my very first prison pen pal girlfriend breakup letter. I could see it coming a while before it happened. My friend was explaining how she would go to weddings, talk about her friends and see herself wanting to get married. The writing was on the wall for me and I realized this might come to an end.

I started reaching different levels of business within the penitentiary ranks, and then out of nowhere I got shipped out. One evening, around November, the CO comes in the middle of the night and says, "Pack your bags Scarborough, you're going to Craggy. I'm like WHAT?! I'm going *back* to Craggy? While I'm packing my bags, making my rounds around the prison to let people know I'm leaving, I think about how I'd be headed back to Craggy as a totally different person than when I first got there in 2011. I'm wiser and more intelligent, so it's gonna be all good, I thought.

* * *

The trip to Craggy was one of the craziest trips of all time. Craggy is only probably an hour or two at the most from Mountain View, however, I had to ride from Spruce Pine in the North Carolina mountains to Sandy Ridge, which is by Greensboro, and all the way back to Asheville to get to Craggy. I'm kind of pissed, because it was a waste of a drive, however, I hadn't been on the bus in about a year. It had probably been like thirteen months since I was last on a transport bus, so it was also a chance for me to see the night sky. I even told this to a CO. I found a way to show gratitude in every little thing, and that was a completely new thing for me. I never had that feeling.

On the way to Craggy, I see some folks from Mountain View. I noticed not a lot had changed since 2011. As a matter of fact, some of the people who were there in 2011 when I left were still there. A few days passed and we had a mail call. I received a letter from my female pen pal, who really had to officially just break it off. Said she wanted to work on things with her ex-boyfriend. She still wanted to communicate as friends. To be honest, I wasn't with all that, so I just left it as it was. I think I said something to her like, "If we can't really communicate to try work on something, I don't want to really talk to you."

That was one of the most painful experiences of my life, because honestly, I didn't have any other options. It wasn't like a breakup in regular society where you can go holler at a girl or find somebody else on social media. I just really felt like, damn, I'm about to do this bid without some type of friend. I had other people write me and be cordial and cool, but none of them were like her. She even sent me money and she drove by herself to visit me. I had a deep place in my heart for her that I had to replace with something totally different. I don't know what happened, but I knew I wanted to do something. I didn't know what the rest of the bid held in store, but I was just prepared for whatever.

Craggy was a younger prison and you had some pretty good basketball talent out there unlike Mountain View. I remember Rabbit would tell me about a kid at Mountain View the year before named Matt from Atlanta, who could hoop real good. He was on Rabbit's team and he won the MVP the year before. Low and behold, I come to the Craggy and Matt's there.

One of the Moorish Science brothers named RaShad Mims-Bey told me about Matt being there.

"Yeah, Matt used to play on Rabbit's team," RaShad said. "He was a former MVP, you the MVP. Y'all need to get it in the yard."

That was funny to me, him trying to schedule a game between me and Matt. We never really got to play that game though. I think he had like a few weeks left on his bid so was going to go home anyway, and I was happy for him.

Basketball wasn't the highest priority on the yard at Craggy, because they didn't really have a gym. Everything was just an open yard. Craggy is where I decided to finally take some classes. I don't even know what classes I took. I was just doing something to keep busy.

The pod I was in was full of younger guys. Some of them were just starting prison, and some just coming to the adult spread. I could really tell a distinct difference, however, I wasn't at Craggy long.

Craggy was a camp with a road squad which gave you the opportunity to bring in drugs. You could bring in any type of drug, weed, tobacco and this other crazy drug called K2. That was big at Craggy. You would see all the white inmates going crazy over this shit. Like going mad berserk. It would have some of them tweaking out, losing their mind, or their cool.

There was this one situation where I was getting ready to get on the phone. I had to go back to my bunk where I left my pen. There was this white guy who went by the name Rooster at my bunk. He picks the pen up off of my bed.

"Hey man this pen looks like mine," Rooster says.

"What?" I say. "No it's not. Stop playing. That's mine. Let me get it back, please. Thank you."

I had no beef with him really.

"Nah man I can show you," Rooster says.

"Aite, man," I say.

I'm entertaining this goofy shit while in my head I'm saying, let him know this isn't his. It's mine, so we can get on about our day."

We get to his bunk and he shows me his pen.

"See you got the same pen," I say. "Great. Now you know it's not yours, it's mine. Now let me have my pen back so I can get on the phone."

Then this motherfucker has the nerve to say, "Nah, dude. I'm keeping it."

I don't know what just happened. I look at him and say, "What?"

"Yeah, I'm keeping it," Rooster says.

After hearing that I really had to process what was happening, because it had crossed the line in my mind to be a joke.

"Ain't no fucking way," I say. I walked up on him. "You said *what?* You think you just gonna take my shit?"

I mushed his head and it bounced off the concrete wall. Then I hear someone say, "Man, yo man. Wait. You got to go to the back and fight him, Justin. Don't do that in front of the block."

So I go to the back and Rooster comes back there with the pen in his hand. I don't know what he's thinking he's going to do with that pen, so the second he got close enough, I just punched him twice in the face. It happened so quickly I really surprised myself.

"Alright, man, damn stop," Rooster says. "I was just playing, man. Fuck!"

"Bruh you don't know me," I say. "I don't know you, so don't play like that."

I was heated, however, a lot of these folks like Rooster were so fucked up in the head. He thought it was cool to play in prison and I was taught by different people. I really had no sympathy. I wasn't even upset about it. The situation made me think, damn, I'm really institutionalized just like everybody else in here.

After this incident, I started being on edge. I tried not to give myself away. The best thing was no one said anything and everyone went on about their day. Nobody did anything because they didn't know anything happened. I punched this guy. I didn't really get into a fight.

I was actually prepared for this incident because something similar happened at Mountain View. I had a cellmate, a little short guy, who just had a big mouth. He didn't know much about prison and folks would pick on him at times. One day he had enough.

"You know what, that motherfucker who keeps messing with me," he tells me. "I'ma goddamn put a lock in a sock and hit him in the head."

You hear these things all the time in prison, so I don't know if he's serious or just wolfing and talking. Then one day, I'm laying in the bed chilling and next thing you know my cellmate and this guy (who nobody really cares too much for) get into an argument. What happened next really was a surprise. My cellmate really hits him in the head with a lock in a sock. A lock in a sock is exactly what you think it is. You put a lock inside a sock and you hit somebody with it. Nine times out of ten, this ends up with someone's head bleeding. When my cellmate hit the guy in the head, the main thing I did was clean up all the blood. I made sure blood wasn't in the craziest areas, got it all wiped up and let's get this shit over with.

When the COs finally came around, I said, "Hey, I don't know what the hell you're talking about." Eventually Sergeant Williams came by. They pulled us out the cell asking what happened.

"Nah, I didn't see anything," I said.

"Well, somebody said someone hit someone with a lock-in-a-sock," she said.

"I didn't see any of that," I said. "Hell, I don't even see blood in the room."

Luckily, it worked. A little blood here and there. I made sure it got wiped up right in time before the COs did their rounds, and I avoided that situation. The next morning and the next few days go on like nothing happened. One particular day, however, I'm in class and I see a sergeant—a *black* sergeant at that. That might have been the first black male I'd seen outside of inmates in probably about fifteen months. He comes into the class and says, "Scarborough, come outside."

The moment I'm outside the classroom he says, "Submit to the cuffs."

"What the hell is going on," I said.

"So you don't know what's going on?"

"Nah," I said. "What's up?"

Of course, I had a feeling why he was there, but I wasn't sure. They might know something I don't know. They might know something I do know, but I wasn't about to tell him.

"What's up?" I ask again.

"Let's keep going."

They take me to the hole. The same damn hole I was in during 2011. I say to myself, well ain't this some shit. Once I entered the hole, I noticed no other inmates were back there. It took them forever, but they eventually brought some food back. I still wondered what was going on and if they had any explanations.

Luckily, I had my radio and I could hear one of my favorite TV shows, *American Horror Story*. A day or so passed before the sergeant came by.

"Hey man, you assaulted that poor boy," he said.

"I don't even know what the hell you talking about," I said. "What do you mean assault?"

"You attacked him," he said.

"Does it *look* like I attacked him? Or do y'all not have any audio?"

"Well..." he said.

"Well," I said. "Let's be perfectly clear. Did you not see him approach me with an instrument in his hand? I didn't know what the hell he was going to do. What am I supposed to do, just sit there and wait for it?"

Like always, I found myself to be a bit witty when it came to COs. There were a lot of neat things I learned about COs at Mountain View and this was one of them. I learned how to get as minimum punishment as possible. A guy at Mountain View by the name of Dwight Clark was the resident superintendent. You could tell Clark with just an overall ass, but he was alright, I guess. At one point I got in trouble for having someone's family member send me money for a debt they owed for the canteen. Once they paid it, the COs could tell there was a conflict. They noticed the same names were on two different order forms. This was an immediate red flag, because we were not related and they wrote me up. I already had one previous write up on my record, so this was going to be number two.

With Clark, however, I was able to get it suspended. I don't know what I told him. I think I told him something like I knew the other inmate and his mom before coming to prison, we kind of grew up together, even though he was like forty years old. My story was that I knew more of his little brother and the mom just sent me some money. Surprisingly enough, they just let it pass. I lost my job, they charged me some money to my account, and that was that.

At Craggy, I could feel this time it was going to be different. I told the sergeant that I was defending myself, but he said he couldn't let me back on the yard.

"What if you start a race war?" he said.

"When in American history have you known for black people to start a race war? Besides, motherfucking *y'all* will probably win. You outnumber us anyway. I highly doubt a race war will happen. It wasn't anything racial. He just rolled up on me with a pen."

The sergeant dismissed the idea and left. What took place next was what really surprised me. It was Thursday night and I woke up after listening to a great evening of *American Horror Story.* I get a knock on my cell door and hear someone say, "Scarborough, pack your shit."

"Where am I going?" I ask.

"Caledonia."

"WHAT?!"

Let's share a little bit of history on Caledonia. The place is legendary in the North Carolina prison system and rumored to have been one of the first slave prisons in the state. They call it, The Farm. It was known to be real violent, real gangster and real black. I guess this was going to be their way of teaching me a lesson. They were probably thinking something like, yeah, we had you pampered up here in the mountains and now were going to send you out toward the coast. In my mind, it's the same damn prison wherever. It didn't matter if the prison was next door to my house or six hours away. I still can't leave until 2014.

I wake up the next morning and get ready to leave. It's my first time ever being shipped out of a prison from a write up. Basically, the lieutenant told me they were kicking me off the yard and I was never allowed to come back. I guess he thought he was kicking me out of a country club or something. Like that was such a big, big terrible thing. I'm like, good, I got kicked off a prison yard. This was the mindset of Justin at age twenty-three.

As I get on the transport bus, another officer says to me, "You need to watch yourself. Caledonia is pretty rough. It's kind of dangerous."

"Listen," I said. "It's going be the same thing wherever I go."

The ride there was more excruciating than any ride I'd ever been a part of, because this one took forever. I was going from one end of the state to the other. Surprisingly enough, you always get there by 6 p.m. I don't know how they do this, but they always seem to pull it off.

My stay at Craggy was short again, thank the good Lord. Now I was embarking on a new journey at Caledonia, and this was going to be one for the ages.

Caledonia

We finally arrive at Caledonia and you can instantly tell it's one of the oldest prisons in North Carolina. It felt like we had gone back in time or something. I knew this camp was different because when I got off the bus the first thing I noticed was nothing but black COs.

Even on the ride there, you could hear guys say, "Boy, they got some girls at Caledonia. They got some women COs. You can do some good time at Caledonia. They'll treat you good out there." Alright, I thought, we going to see about that.

When I get off the bus at Caledonia, the sergeant doesn't tell me that strip off my clothes, squat and cough, hold my testicles, or any of that degrading shit. The sergeant asks me how I'm doing and I say I'm good. He pats me down like security would at a club, then—this part is what really blew my mind—he helped me take my bags to the cell. I say to myself, what the hell is this? I never received this much courtesy since being in prison. It was definitely an eye-opener.

As I walked further into the prison, I could see that, just as the guys on the bus said, they definitely had women there. On the way to my block, I realize that this is indeed a very old-school prison. No cameras like Mountain View, only mirrors and the COs still used a key to open the gate to the block. It was very astonishing.

I finally make it to my block and I see nothing but black guys. I thought, cool. Caledonia had a different set of rules, although the inmates and the prison itself was supremely old school. Outside of being in the hole, I never had my own room. That was until I was at Caledonia.

At Caledonia they let you watch all types of TV programming, from Fused, MTV, BET to all the good stuff. At Mountain View, we didn't get none of that, only sports. Mountain View was a big sports camp.

You see a lot more people that look like you. Caledonia was also heavily influenced by gangs. It was almost like an older version of Polk Youth Center.

What was real funny was on my first day at Caledonia I walked into the block and this dude from Brooklyn confronted me.

"Ayo, you hoop? With your big-ass feet," he said.

"Yeah," I said.

"Yo, you nice or what? I mean, what the fuck. You nice or what?"

"Yeah, I'm nice," I answered. "I can hoop."

"Alright, we gone see," he says. "We're going to see then nigga."

I laugh.

"Alright."

Caledonia was like the hood and it was straight. My first real lesson at Caledonia I remember sitting down walking out the cell to sit down in the day room to watch TV and I have on some shower shoes.

"Aye, man," someone said. What the fuck you doing wearing your shower shoes in the day room? What the hell prison did you come from?"

"Bruh, I came from Mountain View," I said.

"Bruh, hell nah," he said. "You can't do that shit here, bruh. You better wear shoes in the day room. You can only wear those shower shoes in the shower. Don't wear them shits in the day room."

In my head I'm thinking like, man relax, but I notice everybody there had their shoes on in the day room. They had their shoes on always. This opened my eyes to realize like, damn, what type of camp was I at before? Most of the dudes at Caledonia had done some time in closed custody. Closed custody facilities are a higher level of security. They are more strict, more dangerous. After closed custody, you have super max and then death row.

This was one of my first lessons. I said to myself, at this camp, you always on guard. *Always* on guard. Not a moment could pass that I wasn't on guard. For instance, say you get into an argument, and it quickly turns into a fight. If you have on shower shoes, you're at a severe disadvantage.

Orca Moment: Remember to plan for the small details. Whether they happen or not, at least you're already mentally prepared. This just wasn't just true in prison, but everything in life, especially when reaching for goals. A lot of people have vision boards, but never envision the details it takes to get there.

So my first time at Caledonia was my introduction to what it was like to be at a majority black, gang-filled prison yard. Caledonia was definitely alright, but it was starting to get real. A few days later I played my very first basketball game on the yard at Caledonia. Before we played, I asked Brooklyn if BuShawn was there.

"Yeah he's here," Brooklyn said. "He be hoopin. He gone be out there, you're going to see him. He's on this side of the prison."

"Cool." I said.

Once we hit the yard, I noticed Caledonia had even more hoopers than I thought. Luckily, I was training before I got there, so I was ready for the level of competition. One thing Brooklyn said, in his thick New Yorker accent, was "Caledonia got them shooters, B!"

There was an old man there by the name of Phil who was like sixty-some years old. He could make three-pointer, after three-pointer, after three-pointer. I was like, what?! We had BuShawn out there who's a penitentiary legend of the court his damn self, and there was Brooklyn.

Brooklyn was a certified New York dude straight up and down. Brooklyn had nice handles and had a nice passing game. It was like, damn it's a shame this man is in prison. He had a certified 'up north' game and it spoke volumes. I could tell he could pass so well that I just always had to have my hands out and ready. He was a playmaker and it showed.

Caledonia was already showing signs that I was about to be in for the time of my life. My first few days of Caledonia was of course adjusting to the prison yard, as usual. In the back of my head, I was happier than most because now I'm approaching 2013 and I'm thinking, man, hell yeah. I got one year left and I'll be outta here. I get to do this prison time around black people. Even though the COs were still the COs, they were black. Some of them were cool. It was a bit of a relief to be in prison around people who look like you. I know that sounds terrible, but it is what it is.

While still getting adjusted to Caledonia life I remember what every prison yard has in common: gambling, gambling, and more gambling. One thing I knew was that gamble is common ground in any prison.

The skills I learned at Mountain View, I applied at Caledonia. I noticed instantly the Caledonia was very different. I guess loose is the word I'd use to describe the environment. It's so loose that you can see people doing anything on the prison yard. It was almost unimaginable. When I noticed just how loose it was, I went around asking, who got tickets, who had to parlay tickets. At Caledonia they have a different level of parlay tickets.

For those of who don't know, a parlay is very different from pick of the week. Parlay is where you place money on points, who's going to win and by how many or whatever. Once I found out who had the tickets, I found out that these parlay tickets at this prison camp were loose—and I mean real loose. The parlays were so loose at Caledonia that I hit for four weeks in a row. It was crazy. Some would believe that I'm responsible for making tighter spreads on their parlays. They were too easy at Caledonia when I first got there.

* * *

I'd been at Caledonia a few weeks or and I was starting to really like the single-room set up I had. Even though people were telling me not to get comfortable, it was hard not to. I wanted to stay there badly, but as usual, I wasn't up for taking a class. Also, the job backlog was so crazy, it was almost insane. Eventually my time on the One Side block came to an end. One of the COs came to my door and said, "pack your stuff. You going to Two Side." Two Side was an open dorm, a very traditional prison. Two Side had real bars, and it made you feel like you were locked up.

Caledonia was another work camp. You can't be at Caledonia and do nothing. They did not play that. You had to be doing something. You were going to go to school, or you were going to work if you wanted to be on One and Two Side. I didn't do either for a while. I got lucky and got moved to one block on Two Side that was for guys who weren't working or in school. You were just doing time.

I did hit the yard, however, work out and train. Caledonia allowed you to train in many different ways. Mountain View is what made me conscious of who I am, but Caledonia made me god— in terms of really mastering who I am and who I wanted to become.

One day I met someone who was from Charlotte. He'd been locked up a long time. We called him OD. He was a light-skin dude. I think he'd been locked up like twenty years. He was like nineteen when he went in and by then he was like forty. He asked me the traditional questions, where you from, what's your name? Blah, blah blah, and I answered accordingly. He seemed like he had been locked down awhile. It's hard to believe that you have people who have been in prison pretty much their whole entire life. OD wasn't much for words at that time. He was just making an introduction.

C block was very tight, and by tight I mean in terms of physical space. The entire block seemed like it was the size of a high school boys locker room, with twenty beds, with a bottom and top bunk. There was only one shower head so you had to pick a time to shower when most people aren't even thinking about showering.

My first day in C block, we had gym call. This is when I learned how different Caledonia truly was. Walking into the gym I noticed they had a punching bag, and dudes actually learned how to box. It intrigued me because ever since I was a child I wanted to box. My mom wouldn't let me box. She probably thought I'd end up looking like the people Mike Tyson knocked out instead of being Mike Tyson. She allowed me to participate in karate, but I didn't like karate. I wanted to box.

The entire gym call, I'm watching OD train, hit the bag, work the mitts, even do some conditioning. I think to myself like, yo, I want to get into this. I really want to get into this. So, I try to holler at my homeboy OD for the longest. I'm like, "Yo man, what's up? You gonna train me or what, man?"

"I don't do no training man," he said. "I can teach you a little bit, but I don't train like that man."

Even after he told me that, I kept antagonizing him. OD just kept laughing me off, until one day I guess he had enough of it and he ran up on me and said, "Put your hands up." I have to be honest, he low-key whooped my ass.

Afterward he said, "Alright, I'm gonna take you to my homeboy man, I'm gonna take you to the dude who show me how to box." I think to myself, what the fuck was this? Some type of initiation or something? However, I really didn't care. I wanted to learn how to box, and if an ass-whooping was what it took to see if I'm for real, then so be it.

"Cool. That's what's up," I said. "I'm with that."

The next day we go to the yard and OD said, "Hey Kirk. Yo, man this is Justin. We call him Slim."

That's what they called me in Mountain View, but your nickname tends to change from prison to prison. They called me Slim.

"Yeah man, this is Slim," OD said. "He's been over here nagging me about boxing, so I thought I'd bring them to you."

Now, I was in One Side in the block with Kirk and I never knew this old man here could actually fight. It was just another one of those eye-opening situations where you realize like, damn, you don't know who you're dealing with in prison. Kirk was probably one of the top five boxing fighters on the North Carolina state prison yard.

You're probably thinking, how is that possible? Well, in prison when you're locked up over a certain amount of years like ten or fifteen, you do a lot of traveling to different prisons. You build yourself a name, especially as a fighter, and for the guys that could box, it's like their name lives on forever from prison to prison. Kirk was well respected, so you know, that respect had to be earned.

By now Kirk was like in his fifties and was a very peaceful dude, but he could whoop ass. For the longest I was shocked.

"OK, I'm going to train you," Kirk said.

I was so excited. I'm like, yeah, finally I can learn how to box! It was almost a childhood dream of mine. Now, granted we were still playing basketball on the yard and working out, but I was excited to learn how to box.

My very first day training Kirk tells me he wants me to work on balance, balancing my body and having balance of myself. I'm telling myself whatever this man said to do, I'm willing to do. Period. I was always coachable and I knew listening was going to be the key for me to excel quickly.

That very first day we didn't even throw punches or anything. He teaches me how to bounce myself on one leg, shows me how to balance myself doing various stretches. Even as a grown man, he shows me how to do a handstand. He actually did one himself—at fifty years old. Then it was my turn to do one, and I think I fell on my face and then fell on my back. I fell at least a hundred times trying to do a handstand for several days. I asked Kirk why this was important. He said he wanted to show me the importance of having balance in your body and how it will play out in my everyday life. I started noticing quickly how boxing was going to be a life teacher as well. Balance and practicing balance on a daily basis was my first piece of instruction before I threw any punches.

In Kirk's mind, the first way to become a great fighter is to have balance. He said we're going to start from the bottom and work our way up. The next thing Kirk wanted to work on was how to move my feet. On the yard at Caledonia, there was a volleyball pit full of sand. Kirk told me to take off my shoes. We would practice me moving my feet in the sand. Moving around left to right, right to left, in a circle, forward and backward. He showed me a figure eight motion and how to get my feet together. I focused on my feet a lot with Kirk. It would be times I would go out and you just see me somewhat prancing around the yard 24/7. Working on my feet was a major thing.

We kept this up for a while, and he finally got to showing me the jab, the right hand, what we called the two, and the left hook. I was out there every day training, training and doing more training. While working out with Kirk, I noticed there was another group of fighters out there, or what's called a stable.

The stable was run by guys named Magnetic and Imjhaid. I thought to myself, well, damn, Caledonia has a yard full of fighters out here, which was dope. Caledonia allowed you to actually train people how to box. It was almost unreal to me. Mountain View wouldn't dare let this go down. It was almost like Caledonia, in its own way, allowed you to work off the stress that came with being in prison.

One morning I woke up ready to hit the yard and start training again. I got outside and waited for Kirk. A few minutes pass, and Kirk never comes. This one dude named Tim came to give me the news.

"Slim, I got to tell you the truth, man. Kirk, got shipped out last night."

I was so hurt. I felt like something was snatched from me. I felt like there was a moment where I wasn't going to be able to get better in boxing. However, I was still a part of the Moorish Science Temple and the grand sheik at the time approached me and said, "Never look at situations like this as a negative. In the eyes of the universe, Allah, you're now ready for the next level. The master only appears when the student is ready."

I didn't really understand what the hell it all meant at that time, however, I never took these things lightly. I just allowed them to manifest. Even though Kirk left, I kept doing. I kept going out there. I kept working out, trying things on my own and realized I was probably out there fucking up terribly.

One day, I'm working out, and I hear Magnetic who very much was a beast at boxing, say to me, "You keep on looping that damn hook, you going to get hit in the fucking face."

"What?" I said.

"If you keep on looping that hook, you're going to get hit in the fucking face."

"Well, show me how *not* to loop the hook then."

"I'm working out, but I'm going to get up with you. Don't worry about it."

And what the grand sheik said suddenly made sense.

Orca Moment: *The universe, God, Allah, Jesus—whatever fits you—knows exactly when you are ready to ascend to the next level, and the correct people who can help you will always be around. You have to be ready, though, you have to be open. You have to be coachable. There's nothing wrong with not being able to do it all by yourself.*

The moment Magnetic told me that, I felt a different type of excitement. Magnetic was a different type of person, however, I was again ready for whatever came my way. Magnetic told me he would train me, and my boxing journey in prison was about to continue. This was going to be a great ride.

The Sergeant

Befrore we started training, Magnetic would say, "I'll train you, but if I train you, you also got to work out with my little bro, Imjhaid, who is Muslim."

He was a white guy, but it was different. He was very, very different. He never used his privilege to his advantage, to say the least. He was a good kind-hearted dude, a good spiritual dude. So I told Magnetic, "Alright, that's cool. I'm with it. I'm here for whatever. We can do that."

It was set for us to train, however they were all on One Side. It was kind of hard for me to catch them on the yard at the same time I was on the yard. I had like a year and some change left on my bid, so I was going to try to do as much as I could until then. I just knew it was going to be a bit of a stretch to catch them. We didn't have gym when they did, so hitting the bag and the mitts was going to be a stretch as well.

One day I see Magnetic get sent to Two Side, the open-door side of Caledonia where I was stationed. That moment, I started to really realize the power of manifestation and really trusting what takes place is always for your betterment when you put the correct energy into the world.

Magnetic moved in later in the evening. With Magnetic over on Two Side, you could tell the mood of the prison yard kind of shifted. I wasn't sure why, but Magnetic was very much a power player on a different level. He was a member of The Nations of God and Earth and he possessed a different type

107

of next-level type of knowledge. It was similar to Moorish Science and a lot of those guys were in the Nation of God and Earth too.

One day I'm lying in my bunk. I have a bunk near the bars, and Magnetic comes, wakes me from my sleep and says, "Yo, what's up? You trying to go put in some work?"

"Hell yeah," I say.

"Alright. Let's go."

So I hop up out of my bunk and head to the yard. It's not too many people out in the yard this morning. Once I got out there, I did some stretching and I said I'm ready.

"Alright, get on your toes," Magnetic said.

He showed me this drill. I remember watching him do this exercise with the other guys plenty of times, and I'm thinking, this is going to be simple. I'm on my toes, bouncing on my feet, but Magnetic says, "No, I want you to be up and down on your ankles, but I don't want your ankles to waggle. I want you to build up those small muscles in your feet."

I saw his fighters do this a lot, and I heard a lot of people criticize it, but you know, if I hear criticism, that means something great is taking place. I learned this at Mountain View: When people criticize what you're doing—and they aren't attempting it all—it usually means they don't know why something works. They're condemning, because they don't understand.

While I'm doing this drill, my fucking calves are burning. We went to working on some more footwork drills, and I had to be in a boxing stance. I lunge forward, pushing off my back foot then going back, pushing backward pushing off my front foot.

"Kirk did a great job focusing on your feet first," Magnetic said. "You just got to pick up your speed."

While he's saying this my calves are still on fire, but I knew that if there was pain, that's where you need to be. Not an injury type of pain but like soreness. I told myself, we were working on our bodies on a different level now and this is where we need to be.

I started enjoying being uncomfortable. I knew even though I felt a little pain, that's where I need to be. On the other side of pain is magnificent growth. This wasn't only a message for working out, or boxing, but life in general. I slowly started noticing the type of mental toughness it took to really be successful in the real world.

We did this day in, and day out, work on my feet, work on my legs. I noticed how much improvement it made in my overall athletic ability, especially in basketball and running. We still had the gym calls, and the guys would want me to play basketball, but boxing had taken over my mind.

Before training with Magnetic, I sparred with a guy on our block named Shaka. One time, when we were doing some light sparring, he caught the best of me several times. I didn't really appreciate that but that's just what boxing was about. I noticed he didn't train how I did. He trained with OD, and it was just something to do for him. That was an advantage I noticed I had over him. Some people don't have the drive to continue something, especially if they're not committed.

Orca Moment: Commitment is the key to reaching any type of success. Being committed beyond traditional reason is what you need to learn any new skill faster. Committing yourself to the entire process, especially the downs, will bring you the results you want.

During my time at Caledonia, I met a homeboy named TJ who was from Charlotte. TJ was originally from Florida and was a great dude. He was a great-hearted dude always willing to hustle. He was just always hustling, always hustling. Now, there were rumors that TJ was also a boxer. I didn't know this. I didn't realize it until then, but Caledonia was a big fighting camp. TJ would say, "Hey man, I see you out there training, bruh. You be putting in that work, you're going to be good. You're going to be good."

I would really appreciate that. Words of encouragement were always good, especially from people who actually knew what they were talking about. It's always good to surround yourself with people who speak positive words to you, especially while you're doing any type of personal development.

Working out with Kirk was extremely different from working out with Magnetic. The only time I was able to really punch was either punch the air or punch the bag. Magnetic was a different level of insane—one that I appreciated. One time Magnetic gave me a pound with his fists and his knuckles were hard as bricks.

"I want that," I told him. "I want my hands to be like that."

"You do?" he said.

"Yeah."

"Alright."

The next yard call, we go workout and work on the jab. On the yard, we only had basketball goals, weights and the pull-up bar. The basketball goals had a blue pad around them, and on the other side of that pad was a steel-like metal beam holding up the rim. That's what we used as punching bags. We put on garden gloves to act like a little ace bandage or wrap a sock around our knuckles and that's how we punched. We punched this bag, this pole, day in and day out. We punched it in the rain, punched it in the snow. I remember punching this pole so much that my hand got swollen. I wasn't able to write a letter for about five days, almost a week. All I could do was call my family on the phone, but I enjoyed the process of becoming a fighter.

Then there was strength and condition with Imjhaid. That in itself was life-changing. I became addicted to high-intensity, full-body workouts. I was already pretty good at dips and pull-ups, but working out with Imjhaid and the other guys took me to a different level. We would do duck walks, alligator crawls, bear walks on our knuckles on the concrete, push-ups on our knuckles on gravel, lift crazy weights. We didn't lift a lot of heavy weights, but we did crazy exercises, with a lot of reps, and a crazy amount of running.

All of it was just on a different level than anything I had ever experienced before, and I was really coming to understand what it meant to be a boxer. It wasn't like basketball training, which was easy for me. It was exhilarating to know you can push your body to this level and I wanted more of it. It was like a drug. I wanted more, I wanted more, I wanted more. I wanted to use my time as best I could training for boxing.

I reached another level in creating my own freedom. I started noticing I had freedom of my own time and could create what my time actually looked like.

Orca Moment: Noticing the value of your time and proper relationships. Trust the process no matter how painful it gets.

I started looking at prison as almost like a gift as opposed to a punishment, even though there were still the ups and downs of being in prison. I remember what my homeboy Man said when I first got to Craggy.

"You take prison serious," he said. "This is a serious experience. Make it a learning experience, and you take the best from it."

I really started noticing that's why I was living. It was not surprising to me that the best part of prison was near the end of my bid. Things started changing. Like I said, Caledonia is a working camp. You don't work, you don't eat. There was this sergeant there named Sergeant Gatlin. I promise you he used to get on my damn nerves all the time. He was all right, though. There was something about him that you could tell he wanted the best for you, but he couldn't necessarily show it. He didn't take no shit. He was an old-school guy, he didn't mind telling you what he thought.

"Boy, listen. You about to go over there and work," he told me. "I see you throwing some punches. Hell, if you don't get you a goddamn job, you're gonna be on Three Side fighting. I think you'll survive though, Scarborough. Shit, you look good with that jab and that one, two, but I'll tell you right now, you better get your ass a goddamn job."

I looked at him and said, "Bruh, what the fuck? Y'all don't have any jobs."

"Don't worry," he said. "I got something for you."

And he actually did. It was called The Kitchen.

So I'd been at Caledonia for several months, but before I went to the kitchen, some next-level events took place. This is how I knew that the money wave was very real. At one point in C block everyone had a real go-getter attitude. Everyone had something going on.

Then this guy from New York gets shipped to Caledonia and assigned to our block. You can tell this individual is different. Matter of fact, he was probably the realest gangster I ever met in my goddamn life. He went by the name Johnny. He had that aura like he was one of those guys you hear about on drug documentaries, the kind with a crazy rap sheet of crimes and prison time. He ended up being my bunkmate. Now, for the life of me I don't know why these types of people are sent my way, but I truly believe there is no such thing as coincidence.

As he approached the bunk, he says this in a very NYC accent:

"Aye, yo. You my bunkie?"

"Yeah," I say.

"Alright, yo you got food? You good?"

"I'm pretty straight," I say.

"Yo, don't worry about it," he says. "We going eat. Trust me, we're going to eat."

Now you hear about these New York-type hustlers in movies and shit and read about them in books, but I never really ran across one, until I met this dude. Now in this block we have Magnetic, Johnny, OD and Shaka. This block is turning out to be very, very supreme.

A few days passed and we're talking about the crimes we committed to get into prison. I told him how much time I had left and then he told me about his.

"I got five life sentences."

"What the fuck? What are you even doing here," I say. "You sharing bunks and you have five life sentences?"

"Yo man," he says. I'm working on getting out."

"OK, how?" I ask.

One thing I wasn't going to do was discredit what he was saying, because one thing I'd learned in all this was anything is possible.

"Just by hustling shit," Johnny says. "I'm a hustle up this money, buy me a lawyer, probably Bill Cunningham next-thing shit. I'm gonna get my time reduced."

I mean, he had it all planned out. I told him I believed him, and a part of me actually did. Years later, once I got out of prison, I looked up Johnny's record. He was still in prison, however, he did, in fact, manage to get some of his sentences dropped.

One day, Johnny asked me if I wanted to try to hustle something. I told him, "Bro, I'm always down to hustle something. I don't give a damn about it."

He handed me some cigarettes. I don't know how he got them inside the prison, because cigarettes at this time were illegal on the prison yard. North Carolina had passed a bill that banned smoking indoors and it ended cigarettes being sold in prison. Johnny somehow got the cigarettes in and we sold them on the yard. Johnny gave them to me to sell, and I would bring him back twenty percent of whatever I sold.

We took a Newport pack and broke it into thirds and sold them for like two dollars. That might not sound like much, however, in prison those dollars started adding up and going a very long way. Once the word was out that we had the cigarettes, it was pretty easy to sell out, because everybody smoked cigarettes—and I do mean everyone.

We had this hustle going for quite awhile. Caledonia COs weren't like Mountain View COs. They didn't throw a fit if you were smoking cigarettes. As long as you weren't killing someone, they didn't care too much about anything.

After a few weeks, someone else moved to the block, a dude from Durham who went by the name TC. Johnny and TC had known each other from a previous prison. TC had major rank in the Folk Gang. He had the highest rank on the yard for the Folk. He ended up also being in C block with the rest of us.

He went to Johnny, and pointed at me and said, "Yo, this yo mans?" (Meaning are we cool? Do we know each other?)

Johnny said, "Yeah, he good. We good."

Meanwhile, I'm thinking, what the fuck we 'bout to get into now? Listening to their conversations I notice Johnny and TC are thinking 24/7 about getting money. For that, the Caledonia yard was the best place to be in North Carolina. "I've been scouting out Caledonia for years," Johnny said. "It just took me a while to get here, because I had to work down my points from closed custody. I always keep a splinter (prison knife) on me and one time they found one. It really set me back."

"Do you have one on you now?" I asked.

He then proceeded to pull up his pant leg and showed me the craziest knife I'd ever seen. He told me he made it himself with a piece of metal, hot water, and a crack in the concrete. He kept chiseling away at it until it was sharp. That wast first time I was ever told the process of making a prison knife, and I was surprised on how simple it was to do.

"So wait, you just scout out prison camps?" I asked.

"I always do this," Johnny said. I'm a lifer. I need to find out where it's sweet so I can make the best use of my time."

"Wow," I said.

After a few days, I don't know how, but I ended up striking up a conversation with TC. He shared with me how he got sentenced to thirty years at the age of twenty-two. He had been in prison for eight years already. There were rumors on the yard that he shot a cop, and that's how he got so much time. Those rumors turned out to be true. That same day he told me something else I didn't immediately believe.

"I'm about to get a phone in here, boy," he said.

"You not getting no damn phone in here," I said.

"Alright, watch," he replied. "I'm going to have a phone in here. You can hold it down if you want to."

I said, alright, but in my head I thought, we're going to see about that shit.

The next day was Saturday, visitation day, and TC came back from a visit. True enough, he came back with a cellphone, a small little flip phone, but on the yard it was like the holy grail. When he showed me the phone, I think my eyes might have slightly popped out my head. All I could hear was Rabbit in my head saying, "The most important thing you need to do is always conduct yourself like you're handling business. Watch how you carry yourself because it's always eyes watching. No matter what you think, someone's always watching."

Once we got this cell phone in the block, I changed how I did a lot of things. Number one was my overall movement. Having a cellphone in prison is a very big deal. It gave me access to talk to anybody I wanted to. I remember the day I started using a phone, it was May 12, 2013. I had exactly one year until I was going to go home.

The closer I got to my release date, the riskier it would get for me if I got into trouble, and that cell phone was something serious. I called all the people I knew. I called my mom, people I went to school with, people that I was writing letters to on a regular basis. Most people were surprised, and would say things like, "Damn, you got a phone? You got a phone? That's what's up."

I was so addicted to using that phone that my day consisted of working out and going right back to the block, laying down and being on the phone. Everyone in the block would say, "Damn, man. You going to get out the bed?" I replied back with something like, "Nah, man. I don't feel good today." I was lying like hell. For me it was all about using this phone, texting, trying to find a female to holler at, and possibly have someone to look forward to when I came home from prison. Seeing that I was single, I knew the time was near where women might be open to the idea of finishing the last twelve months of my bid with me, but that endeavor of mine was about to be cut short.

One day there was a raid in the block, and I had the phone. My entire thought process was to hide the phone so we could keep using it, so I hid it somewhere I thought it was going to be safe. Luckily, when the COs came in the block I was already in a position to hide the phone, but it's like the COs knew exactly where to go find it. This is how I knew somebody was watching at all times.

What the hell? I thought. They found where I hid the phone, then they snatched TC out the block and took him to the hole. That was even more surprising than them coming in the block to me. They didn't do any type of investigation. If it was their plan to take TC, they should have just picked him up in the middle of the hallway or something.

A few days go by after they picked up the phone, they let TC out the hole.

On the yard he came up and asked me, "What the hell happened, bro?" Of course, at first glance, his reaction was that I fucked up.

"To be honest bruh," I responded. "I don't know, but let me ask you this, why the hell did you tell them the phone was yours?"

I never took it like it was all my fault. Did I have a responsibility to play in the phone being picked up? Yeah. I could admit to that, however, I didn't have anything to do with him admitting the phone belonged to him. I told TC that nothing on that phone was incriminating him. Everyone in the block used the phone, so it could have been anyone's phone. There was no reason to want to play hero.

After we had our conversation, he shared that they now had an investigation going and that he would probably get shipped out soon, and that was the end of the run of the cell phone.

Right after that conversation, I ran to my bunk and I sent a letter home to my mom, with a list of numbers I called or texted using that phone. In the letter, I told her the phone had been taken away and that it was part of an investigation. If she saw that number call, I told her don't answer it and don't call it back. I was trying to cover my tracks as best as I could. It seemed to work, and we didn't have any more worries about the phone or COs coming out of nowhere asking if we had any involvement with a cell phone.

All of that was over. The moral of this story is always be on point, and always recognize the money waves when they take place, because they're always bound to take place, and you always have to be ready for them.

Since TC was a big gang member on the yard, I made it my duty to go up to every single last one of his members and explain what happened. I also let them know if they had any problems with what took place, we could handle this shit now. I wasn't going to be walking around prison while people were feeling some type of negative way about what went down and I have to look over my shoulder.

Ironically enough in prison I noticed a lot of those dudes were just here for the ride. They weren't necessarily there to give a damn about what took place. Someone told me, "Man, it's not your responsibility to take care of him."

I said, "What do you mean?"

"Yeah you might have put it in the area, and the COs found it, but it ain't like you told. At the end of the day, he messed himself up. Just keep it moving."

I said, "Alright cool."

I always played it close to the edge in prison, I will say that. I played it *very* close to the edge in prison. I feel like I didn't have anything to lose. I'm already in here. It can't get any worse, however, this was a great learning experience, and it was time for me to move on.

The Kitchen

At Caledonia, since there was such a surplus of women there, everybody was putting on, or doing the most they could to be in front of some woman's face. There were so many women COs and I think it was like a mathematically designed plan that every day you have the opportunity to, "shoot your shot." It was actually something to look forward to. It didn't matter if she was cute, or had a nice body. All that mattered was she was a woman.

Two Side had some good-looking women. However the real beauty was on Three Side. That's all the guys talked about, the women who were on Three Side. It's all Sergeant Gatlin talked about, other than getting a job. I'd wake up first thing in the morning and hear him say, "Yeah, boy you're going to have to get you a job, Scarborough. You ain't gonna be in my unit not goddamn working."

"You really starting to get on my damn nerves with this job shit," I told him. "I really didn't come to prison to work. I came here to do time and get in shape."

"Well, I don't give a damn about none of that," Gatlin said.

I had no choice but to laugh. Gatlin was a funny guy. One day I got a call from Sergeant Gatlin telling me I was going to go to work in the kitchen and report at such and such time.

I said out loud, "Wait, what?! For real?!"

"Yeah, I got your kitchen whites for you," he said. "When you go in there, you're going to report to a Mr. Phillips. Now get your ass up in that kitchen and start working."

I know I had the longest look on my face, I could feel it, however, working in the kitchen was where I was able to tap into my hustle even more. It started becoming just something else to do, something else to add to my routine. I'd work out in the morning, then go to the kitchen at 10 a.m.

Working in the kitchen with something special. I knew a few people who worked there. I was acting like it was something I dreaded, but there was a major flip side to it. What I heard from the kitchen workers at Mountain View was you really can't do much at all but gamble. Caledonia, however, was a lot better.

One of my homeboys in the block was named Stew and another guy from Winston Salem called Southern. Now, Southern could cuss out anybody at the drop of a dime and articulate it perfectly.

Southern and Stew were also the bakers. Stew told me, "Hey man, you'll like the kitchen. You'll be able to get your hustle on, and you look like you like to hustle."

My very first time in the kitchen I worked as a dishwasher, standing in the back in the hot-ass heat. There was hot water, almost like a hundred degrees, to sanitize the dishes, and I was washing dishes all damn day. The guys would come to the line, grab their tray, dump the food, stick the tray in the dishwasher, throw it in the hot water, then let it dry. That was a day-to-day thing.

This was tiring as hell, but it's where everyone started. Eventually, I worked my way up to prep cook, where I cut veggies and cut food for everyone. Now working in the kitchen as a prep cook is where I found out where you could hustle things in the kitchen. At first, I was just in there being naive, but then the hustle came back. I always noticed what happened at particular times of the year.

Orca Moment: I always notice when the money wave was really coming in. I would lean into the wave and ride it for as long as possible, because you never know when it will be that easy again.

One day, I was headed to the kitchen and someone stopped me.

"Aye, Six-O, can you get me an onion?" he asked.

"Get an onion? How am I going to get it out?"

"Either pass it through the bar, or sneak it out," he said.

"Bruh, I don't know how to do none of that, yet."

One day I asked Stew and Southern how to sneak items out of the kitchen.

"Listen here man," they said. "All you got to do is wrap that motherfucker."

"Wrap? What do you mean?"

So watched Stew and Southern put plate-sized portions of food onto some shrink wrap, wrap that food so tight, take it out and then just hide it between their legs or crazy places when they were leaving. I was like, "Yo, it's really that easy."

When they showed me that, I learned the art of hustling out of the kitchen. One of the things about me in prison, if I saw something that looked sweet, I was about to lean in and I wasn't going to play about it. I said to myself, let's go ahead and lean in like we do with everything else.

After becoming a prep cook, I worked myself to what they called one of the greatest jobs to ever have in the kitchen, the dietary cook. As the dietary cook you prepare all the diet meals for everyone including people with special diets. The dietary cooks get to prepare some of the best food. We would cook turkey instead of the regular old terrible meat, we had peanut butter, graham crackers and late-night snacks.

People would come to me and say, "Six-O, can you get me a dietary bag? Bag this up for me, and when they call it out, bring it to me and I'll pay you." This was a hustle I would do on a day-to-day basis. It was almost like a five-dollar hustle plus the food that I was eating myself for myself.

Now I actually didn't have to spend too much money. Everything was now almost given to me, but I had to understand just how to make these things work. How do I maximize myself and still be able to live how I want to live in prison?

I always remembered what Rabbit told me, "It's all about how you carry yourself. If you carry yourself like the riff raff, they're gonna treat you like the riff raff. You carry yourself like you're doing business, you'll be able to make as much money as possible."

When I was reading *The Circle Seven* of The Moorish Science Temple of America, it always talked about mastering the higher and the lower self. However, what stood out to me the most was when Prophet Noble Drew Ali said, "it takes finances to build a nation." It takes finances to always be about business, and that's how I operated at Caledonia. I had that same mentality over and over and over and over day by day.

After being the dietary cook for a while, I moved up to a baker job with Stew and Southern. Now, not only was I able to serve peanut butter, but I could also serve cakes. Everyone loved the cakes, especially when Southern baked them. The yard would go crazy when they knew Southern was baking. Everyone would come with their own order and I would send it straight to them through the line. In return, people would give stamps or have items ready for me when I got off from work, so life was pretty good considering where I was.

I could work in the kitchen and still not have to rely too much on money being sent from home. I felt I was doing myself and my family a good service by not asking for money as much, which is why I hustled so hard on the yard.

Dusty Trail

My last year in prison I was working in the kitchen and still working out boxing. A lot of times I thought about what I would do with myself at age twenty-three or twenty-four. I had no clue what was going on in the outside world, and I knew I could do way more with my life than I had over the past three years. I was getting closer and closer to my release, and started to face reality that I really didn't know what was taking place in the real world.

As a twenty-three-year-old, one thing I always appreciated was the eye candy Caledonia hired. They had some of the finest corrections officer women I ever saw. One thing popular at Caledonia was the amount of sexual advances you could make towards women. Sometimes you could cross a line. Some may let you cross that line, some may not. One particular time I crossed that line for sure with Sergeant Warren. This particular incident led me to the hole for eight days.

Going to the hole was another eye-opening experience. A lot of people I knew from the general population were back there. My homeboy TJ was back there as well, and it always surprised me how you can create isolation within isolation. My time in the hole went by kind of slow. I was confined to a cell for twenty-three hours a day. When we were taken outside we had to stay inside a five-foot by five-foot fenced off space. When going to the shower we had to be handcuffed from the cell to the shower. Most days consisted of doing workouts in my room, reading and writing letters home. The hole was a great learning experience and it got my head right. I realized I needed to start seperating from the others who were there. I had to start getting focused on going home, and I needed to let go of institutionalized behavior.

That incident was completely different from when I first got to Caledonia. Now one thing I didn't share yet, was that I was already in trouble. Remember, I got sent to Caledonia because of the fight at Craggy? Well, when I finally went to the hearing at Caledonia, I sat down and wrote out a whole speech I wanted to tell the investigating officer about my incident at Craggy. I explained to him that the situation was something that could have been avoided, I know, but at that moment, you never know what's going to happen. To be perfectly honest, this was the fault of Craggy not wanting to own up to the situation, not y'all (Caledonia). I understand I have to receive some type of punishment for it, but I ain't trying to sit in the hole for thirty to forty-five days over this.

Surprisingly enough he said, OK, man, I understand, and they suspended the sentence. However, I wasn't able to go to the minimum custody facilities. I had to stay in medium custody the rest of my bid. One of the greatest things about going to minimum custody, however, is that you get to have home visits.

I never qualified for the home visits, however, I didn't go back to the hole. I still was able to work, and from then on, all I did was keep my nose clean. He gave me a suspended sentence so things worked out in my favor on that one.

Several months later, I'm back in the same investigation office. I had three write ups, one for every year, and I knew I had passed my suspended sentence time, so I qualified for another suspended sentence. It seemed like the officer didn't even care about the infraction. He told me he was going to suspend the hole time again, and told me to leave.

After my time in hole was up, I was sent to Three Side. Three Side was a lot different than One and Two Side. The dudes over there didn't have jobs, or go to school. They were all about gambling, sports, working out, and chilling. Three Side had a brother by the name of Wise. He was another brother who knew the teachings of Moorish Science, Nations of Gods and Earth, and Nation of Islam. His nickname described him to the T. He was also one of Caledonia's boxer-basketball players on the yard. It was said that he was one of the best basketball players in North Carolina history, and he carried himself like he knew he was.

Wise had taken a real liking to me before I got to Three Side. He heard about me playing basketball, boxing and was very surprised about how I carried myself. When I worked in the kitchen we would talk at the fence and he would share his knowledge with me. I always realized I would attract these types of people, and I loved the fact that I did. I started looking forward to it. He was a cool dude.

When he found out I was on Three Side, he was a little excited, and disappointed because of the reason I was there. I told him what happened and he said, "You not supposed to go to the hole for some shit like that. If anything you're supposed to get caught having sex with a woman CO. I've had sex with enough women on state. You have to be smart about what you do, and don't get caught up with what everyone else is doing. Stay true to yourself."

Wise had the same message as Rabbit and Magnetic: How you carry yourself now, is how you're going to carry yourself when you get out. How do you plan on being different? You may not have it all planned now, but how do you plan on being different?

That was my number one thing. I knew the first thing I had to do was get back in the kitchen and back on One and Two Side. I needed to train and I knew who could pull some strings to get me over there. One day I saw Sergeant Gatlin and I pulled him aside. I told him I was willing to work in the kitchen and asked if he could get me over there. Of course he gave me hell for going to the hole and had to talk shit, but he ended the conversation with, "I'll see what I can do."

A few days passed, and eventually I got back into the kitchen. Gatlin came through on what he said, and I was happy as hell, because I needed to get back to training. I missed out on a lot of training, so when I was able to get back to Two Side and gym day came, Magnetic was ready to train. I was rusty as hell, and it showed in our training, however it was good to be back. I realized how much I loved boxing.

When I got to Two Side, I asked a caseworker what my projected release date was. Surprisingly, I was set for May 12. I realized I had enough points not to have to work in the kitchen. I remembered Mr. Phillips and others saying you can work in the kitchen until you get locked in on your release date. Now, I just wanted to chill and train and I was going to play that card.

The day came when the area superintendent named Mr. Chris called my name to report to the kitchen to work. I told him I was locked in on my release date and I didn't feel like working in the kitchen anymore.

He says, "Scarborough, if you don't report to the kitchen, I'm gonna write you up to send you to the hole."

I looked at him.

"I'll *report* to the kitchen," I said. He looked at me like he knew exactly what I was getting at, because "report" is exactly what I did. I reported to the kitchen, refused to work and then left. I knew that if I reported to the kitchen I would have fallen in line with following orders, however, me refusing to work in the kitchen was outside of Mr. Chris's power to write me up. He knew that. I knew that. I wanted to test the limits.

When Mr. Chris found out I wasn't in the kitchen, he instantly moved me back to Three Side. One thing I always knew in prison was if I knew the rules I could play them how I want. However, he threw a curveball, and I really didn't care about it.

Sergeant Gatlin came by Three Side and said to me, "Scarborough, what the hell do you think you're doing telling a white man you not going to work in prison?"

"I didn't like how he talked to me," I said. "It is what it is."

"Well, I know you want to come back over here so you can punch on that damn pole again."

"So, what do you suggest I do now?"

"I don't know you're smart, you'll figure it out."

And that's exactly what I did.

Caledonia had just hired a new superintendent. I forgot his last name, but his first name was Rick. He had a lot of pull around the state, but definitely in Caledonia. He was the person I knew I was going to talk to, because I remember reading in the book *The 48 Laws of Power*, "when you go for the head, the sheep will follow." He was the superintendent or warden over the entire prison. I wrote him a letter saying something along the lines of, I know I made some mistakes, but I'm trying to get back to Two Side. I want to work, work out with my crew and use this time as wisely as I can.

A couple of days passed and he came to speak with me. He wanted to know how he could help. I was kind of surprised, because I didn't think it would actually work, however I shot my shot at anything in prison. It didn't matter if it was to a female, it didn't matter if it was me writing a letter to see how I could get what I wanted. Fuck it, I had nothing to lose.

Orca Moment: There's nothing wrong with shooting your shot. You just have to get out of the fear in your head thinking it's not going to work. Actually take some action, and you'll be surprised more times than not at the results you will get.

Superintendent Rick explained the process of getting back over to Two Side and he asked if I was willing to work in the kitchen.

"Yeah," I said. "I'm willing to work in the kitchen, man."

"Alright," he said. "I'll tell Mr. Phillips and I'll bring you back."

By the beginning of the next week I was back in the kitchen and back on Two Side. This time, I'm on first shift. I had to wake up at two in the morning to go work in the kitchen, but it wasn't that bad. I was appreciative of the fact I got to wake up early, go to work, and still be on the yard during the daytime when it was sunlight to train and workout. On second shift you don't get to do nothing. Your whole day is taken from you.

During first shift I made breakfast and lunch. Second shift guys just served lunch. As I'm nearing the end of my bid, there's this particular moment where Phillips calls me in the office. He looked at me and said, "Scarborough, what the hell are you doing here?"

"What do you mean? You called me?" I replied.

"No, what the hell are you doing in prison, Scarborough? You don't belong here. I want you to come walk with me to help me get these cans of food."

We walked damn near to the front of the prison and he used this moment to talk to me. As I mentioned before, a lot of people just saw something different in me. It reminded me of what Lavell-Bey at Mountain View told me the day before he left.

"A lot of great black men left prison," he said. "Don't let this be your downfall. You're going to be the next great black man to get up out of here."

While we were waiting on the cans of food Phillips said, "You ain't been this close to freedom in a long time like this have you?"

"Nah," I said.

"Scarborough, you don't belong here, man. I am a good person but some things come with the job. You don't like nor want people like me telling you what to do. You're way smarter than that. I don't know what happened to you, and I don't care, but I never want to see you here again."

"The feeling is mutual," I said.

The day for my release is getting closer and closer. One day I'm walking to the cafe for lunch and another sergeant named Sergeant Scott approached me and said, "This might sound crazy, but it's been a pleasure to meet you. It's been a pleasure to meet you, but it's not a pleasure that you're here. If I ever see you come in here again, I'm gonna take off my badge and I'm going to beat your ass myself. Don't ever come back."

I looked him in his eyes and could tell he meant every word he said.

"You'll never have to worry about me stepping foot in this mothafucka ever again."

It was as if everyone knew it was my time to go, and they were happy about it. Then my trainer, Magnetic, gave me his own thoughts.

"Listen," he said. "You have the ability to do anything you want in the entire world, Justin. You're a great listener. You can do anything. I'm probably more than mad that your parents made you a basketball player instead of a boxer. You might not want to box, you might want to do something totally different with your life, but if I ever see you come back in here again, I will kill you."

And hearing this from a man who committed a murder at a very young age, it was hard not to believe him. One thing I didn't share was that Magnetic was a real boss. He carried himself differently. He was from Boston and was a serious Patriots fan like me, but he approached life very differently. He was a real apex on the yard, a man's man. If he said he was going to do something, he would do it, and if he couldn't do it at that time, he would tell you straight up, and didn't play games.

He would beat your ass. There had been times where me and him would shadow box, and even sparr, and he would really punch the hell out of me. I went through gladiator school with Magnetic. I used to do crazy things. I would do planks and Mag would say, "Do you want your abs to be as hard as steel?"

"Yeah," I'd say.

So I would do planks and he'd kick me on the side in my obliques with his steel-toe boots and I would just sit there. I loved every moment of it because I was being turned to something else.

* * *

When I worked in the kitchen, dudes always loved to play fight. They always wanted to put their hands up to see where they could get and test out their skills for these little ten seconds of life. Like that really meant they could fight.

There was one guy one time who pushed me.

"Yeah, come on come on nigga. Come on nigga what's up?"

I looked and I'm looking around me. I don't know if he's playing around or what, because he does this a lot with younger guys. I was about to stop playing with him whether he was playing or not. So I looked at him, got my hands up and started stepping around him. The whole time he doesn't know I'm forcing his feet to get tangled up. I threw a playful punch and watched my fist shove his lip against his teeth and make his lip bleed.

Ahhh, shit, I thought.

Whatever was supposed to be, even if it started as a joke, just got serious, however I really didn't care.

"Look, I told you stop fucking with me," I told him.

So he tried to pick up a kitchen gadget or something and said, "I'm about to kill this little nigga, man."

"Bruh," I said. "You don't want to do that, because this situation isn't guaranteed to go in your favor."

"Nah, you busted my lip. I'm about to fuck you up."

"Alright."

So he took one more step, I threw the quickest and fastest 1-2 I could at that time. Luckily, he dodged it and then walked out. Like, he walked clean the hell out the room. This would happen every so often. More times was with younger dudes who wanted to test themselves, and I would let them try, because a part of me wanted to hurt them. I loved it. I tapped into a part of myself while I was in prison, especially in Caledonia, where I discovered just how much I am always in control of my own environment. I would tell people, Mountain View made me conscious and Caledonia made me God.

As I finished up my last few days in Caledonia, I thought about how it was now 2014. I had four months left in prison. I told my mom and everybody not to send me any more money. I told my mom in 2013, I didn't need anymore visits from here on out. The next time you're going to see me is when I come home, I said.

However, it wouldn't be a good departure if I didn't shoot my shot at a woman at Caledonia. In my final attempt to shoot my shot, I wrote a letter to the finest CO I'd ever seen in my life. I spent all night writing this letter, explaining how I wanted to take her out when I got out. I really poured it all in that letter. She was the CO on duty in the kitchen, and one day we had to clean up the outside deck area. She had to walk behind us and while we were walking back to the kitchen I made sure I was one of the last guys in the back. I purposely dropped the letter so she could pick it up, but she never did. It was all good, though. I tried and I could hang my hat knowing I tried. I didn't want to cause a scene, so I just left it alone and started thinking about what my life was going to be like outside the prison walls.

Released

As I reached my final night at Caledonia, folks were saying their goodbyes in a very positive but stern way. It was very uplifting to know that people never want to see you come back on this side.

One of the most interesting things was that I didn't go home from Caledonia. It was too far away. I got shipped to my final prison, which was called Salisbury. Salisbury was another prison that was full of black people, but I wasn't really focused on being there. I would still work out, sit in the yard a little bit and chill, but the only thing on my mind was going home.

While I was there, the funniest thing happened. I was standing outside my door for count time and I saw somebody. It was someone I went to college with, a man named Officer Gladden. It was too funny. When he started coming around to do count, I looked at him and said, "Officer, how do you pronounce your last name?"

"Oh shit. Bro, what's up man," he said. "This is crazy."

Traditionally, I am not about mingling with COs, but seeing Marcus as a CO was a confirmation to me from the universe that it was time to get up out of here and go home.

As I was ending my days in prison, I remember looking out the window at Caledonia and I told myself, if I could survive this, I can survive anything. I'm mentally strong enough to do whatever I need to do to reach the level of success I need to reach. I started replaying just how this whole entire process had gone. I had fallen in love with the process of finishing something. I didn't even finish college, but I finished prison.

I remember how it was when I first started boxing, how terrible I started but, how consistently, day by day I got better. I looked at how I started doing pull-ups and dips and how I started so minuscule, like one to two a day, until I was able to do at least a hundred dips and pull-ups every single day.

I had another revelation during my last days in prison was what was really valuable. Before going to prison, I thought it was all about the money, the glitz, the glam, having things come to you quickly, living life all up at once. It wasn't until I was reaching my last days that I realized the greatest thing to have in the world is time.

The value of time is very real. The proper use of time can get you anywhere and get you anything you desire. I stopped believing in everyone else's false views about time and what life should be. I realized, I'm in control of this. When I say Caledonia made me God, I mean that it made me realize that as long as I'm in control of my time, and I am consciously aware of my decisions, I have a higher chance of enjoying the life I wish to live, even when other things come up in life that are outside of our control. I was starting to see how I could structure my life the way I wanted to live it when I got out of prison.

* * *

May 12, 2014: I don't remember how I woke up, all I remember is I woke up and I said to myself, "Damn, the day is finally here. The day is finally here."

I remember going to breakfast and lunch only with the intention of giving my food away to everyone at the table. I told myself the only food I wanted to eat was the food prepared by my mom when I got home. I went back to the block and just laid there savoring every moment before being released.

Then the moment happened. I heard a CO say, "Scarborough, pack your stuff. You getting ready to go home."

I hopped out the bed like a child on Christmas morning. I left everything in there. I didn't take anything with me. I said, bruh, y'all can have all of this. I even left my glasses. I said, "Y'all can keep them shits too. I don't want none of this shit."

I left the block and walked to the processing unit at Salisbury. A CO told me to wait and my post-release officer would come pick me up and take me home.

I was so excited and happy to go home that I didn't even notice I was waiting for what seemed to be like three damn hours. When I looked at the clock, I wasn't even upset. I just did three years, I thought. Three hours ain't shit when I know I'm about to leave.

After three hours of walking around, shadow boxing, reading magazines and thinking about all the people I was going to see when I got to Charlotte, I saw my post-release officer Jacqueline Moore who came to pick me up.

"Scarborough?" she said.

"Yes, ma'am."

"It's time for you to go home."

I remember vividly, walking out wearing these ugly clothes, getting in her car, and driving down 85 South to Charlotte. I already knew the ride was going to take forty-five minutes. That forty-five minutes felt like every bit of ten minutes. All I could think about was going home.

"Your mom's not home right now," she said. "But she will be soon."

She told me how often I had to come to her office for my routine checks and all of this other stuff, but I didn't hear none of that. All I heard was I'm going home.

Going home had to be the greatest experience of my life. When I got out of prison, I knew I had to hit the ground running and stop playing, because I was exactly where I needed to be, *home*.

III

Greatness

*In this part, you will go on a journey to learn how I collected
clues from the world, and others to recognize the difference
between an alpha and the apex*

Home

When I first got home, like my parole officer said, my mama wasn't home. It was cool with me that she wasn't. When I got out the car, I walked so damn slow. I wanted to cherish every single moment. I walked in the door and the house was almost the same. It seemed like things were smaller. I don't know if I got taller in prison, but it felt good being in your own home.

My mom left a note on the refrigerator, telling me there was some food in the microwave. Again, I sat down and ate it *so slow*. It was macaroni and cheese, chicken and some greens. I didn't care what it was, just as long as it was not prison food. Eating my mom's food after coming home from prison was one of the most gratifying experiences I have ever had.

After eating, I found another note where she said, "There's a phone under the pillow. Use the phone." I don't know why she hid it under the pillow, like somebody else was coming in the house, but it was cool. I lifted up the pillow and picked up the phone. It looked like one of the oldest phones. I mean, the phone I had in prison was more up to date, but it didn't matter. Hell, I had a phone. A very traditional phone but it was cool. It was a real humbling moment.

A few hours later my mom got home. We exchanged hugs. I believe she cried and I cried. I don't remember. I don't remember what time she got home, however I know we went to visit people as late as one o'clock in the morning. We went to see her friend Gloria. We went to go see Freddie and his mom at home and these people were awake. That surprised me the most, like wow, all of you are awake at like one in the morning.

My first night home, I didn't go to sleep until about 6 a.m. I stayed up all night. I was on Facebook catching up with people I hadn't talked to in years, getting phone numbers and, of course, doing what all people do when they get home from prison: look for females. I'm not even ashamed to say it. I was like yeah, *where are the women!* That's what I am here for. I was twenty-four years old and hadn't been with a woman in three years. At the same time, I was just thankful and looked for people I could connect with.

My second night home my cousins came to visit me. Shelton, Malik, and his wife Alish came all the way from Fayetteville, North Carolina. Malik and Alisha brought their two children, Jaylen and Aaliyah. That was definitely cool. When they got there, Shelton said, "Hey man, you want to go to Missouri for our family reunion?

"Yeah sure, why not," I said.

I hadn't been up that way in years, but first I had to ask my parole officer if it was OK if I left the state. I went to her office for my first meeting. She was just running things by me like not getting in trouble, going to look for a job, and not smoking any marijuna. After she explained everything I needed to do I asked her if it was OK if I went to a family reunion in Missouri. She said yes. I was very shocked she said yes, mainly because for the last few years all I would hear from people of any authority was mostly no.

When I first got home we didn't have a car. I was dropped off at my parole officer's office and no one was able to pick me up. So I had to walk six miles home. It took me close to two hours to get home. When I started walking, I thought to myself, I used to workout for two hours on the yard everyday, so I know I can make this walk with no problem. It was one of the longest and hottest walks of my life, but I was in great shape. It was a good walk and a hell of an experience. I walked from downtown Charlotte to my house. I was grateful to be home, but I didn't want to get caught up in the thought process of just, oh I'm so happy to be home. Thinking like that would have been the breeding ground for complacency.

I had a lot of those eye-opening moments when I got home. One thing I noticed was how after all this time we were still low on finances. I would think to myself, alright, something's got to give here. I remember one thing Rabbit told me he said, "People think a man is somebody who can go out and stand on the corner all day and trap, but a man is someone who can go out there and apply fo a job everyday and when I tell him no, he still gets up the next day and does it again."

In prison I used to tell myself, "I'm going to try this thing out, whether they tell me yes or no, I'm gonna try this out."

I remember being at home with no money. So I went to job fair, after job fair, and rode the bus all around Charlotte to fill out job applications. One job fair in particular was off of Albemarle Road. I saw a moving company and thought to myself, surely I can get hired by them. It might be rough, but it would be a start. I filled out the application, handed it to the man and he asked me some questions.

"Do you have a driving record within the past three years?"

"No."

"Have you been in an accident in the past three years?"

"No, sir."

"No, traffic tickets either?"

"Nope."

He looked at me as if it was too good to be true. Then came the next question.

"You haven't been locked up have you?"

"Yeah."

"Too bad. I can't hire you."

"What, so I can't even attempt to break my back to work?"

"Nah, man," he said. "We can't hire you."

"Alright," I said.

I got on the bus and went back home. A few weeks went by, and my friend Dairyon said, PF Chang's was hiring and that I should go check them out. That's exactly what I did. I got on the bus to PF Chang's in South Charlotte, filled out an application for the job on the spot and sat down for a little interview. The manager asked me some questions about kitchen experience. I told him I had a year or so of experience. He asked me where and I told him where I worked. Immediately I got denied.

I tried a few more places and got denied all because of my record. Part of me started realizing that this was some bullshit. I asked myself, why the hell am I sitting around here *asking* people and *hoping* they give me a job, knowing damn well I can create any type of economy I want?

I pondered on for a while. Asking for jobs felt like I was doing a disservice to my own brilliance. In the meantime, I kept going, kept seeking some type of employment.

One day I remembered my cousin Courtney wrote me a letter saying he would have a job for me once I got out. So I hit him up, to see what he had going on. He said he didn't have anything at that time, so I just took that as it was and kept moving. I knew he would have something one day. The type of work he did was self-employed, and you had to wait to get called up for assignments.

While I was continuing my job search, I still had a desire to box. My homeboy TJ had a coach at a gym called Charlotte Boxing Academy, so I looked up the gym and asked Freddie if he could give me a ride to the gym. The coach said that the coach who works the adults wasn't there and that I should come back tomorrow.

I went the next day, and still no one was there. I went probably two more times to see what was up. Every time I went to train, no one was there to work with me. I really didn't like the feeling of not being able to work when I showed up to do so. Then I got a call from my homeboy, Vonte. Now, remember Vonte always had an eye for things. He sent me a screenshot of a gym called Dyme Boxing. I looked them up, found them on Facebook, and said to myself, "Alright, this might be the move."

They weren't advertised to people who weren't on their game. They looked like they knew what they were doing. So I made the call to talk to Coach Presley, the head coach at Dyme, who told me to come up there when I could. I told him I would. After talking to him, I knew I was making the correct decision to go to Dyme Boxing.

Dyme Boxing

The first time I walked into Dyme Boxing it was a surreal experience. I had never been to a real boxing gym outside of what I saw at Caledonia, and that was just a bag. Before leaving, Magnetic said you don't want to go to no pretty boxing gym. You want to go to a gym where it looks like it's war in there.

Dyme was housed in an old warehouse off of South Boulevard, but it gave off the feeling of a dungeon. They had three different boxing rings, which was dope. On the other side of the building they had a mixed martial arts gym.

My first day there coach Smoove said, "I heard you were coming. We're about to go run three miles."

"Word," I said.

"Yeah, three miles to Tyvola and back."

I knew I was in shape. I ran a little bit in prison sometimes, but I don't know if it was three miles. The moment he told me the destination I took off and started running and it was like it was pretty cool. It wasn't as bad as I thought it was going to be. I wasn't trying to leave people, but I definitely left some folks.

After running three miles, we went to hit the bag. Smoove asked me how long I had been boxing.

"Maybe a year," I said. "I learned how to box my last year in prison."

"Alright, that's cool," he said. "Bernard Hopkins learned how to box in prison too."

We continued to have a conversation, however he was letting me know that this is where I needed to be for boxing. I could tell he was impressed by how I showed up to the gym. After hitting the bag a few rounds, I started watching the other fighters spar. That's when I realized, yo, this thing is kind of real.

I'm trying to do my best to size folks up, but at the end of the day, I'd only been hitting some pads. I hadn't yet begun sparring, but that's why I was at Dyme.

I noticed very early on there was one guy who was one of the best at the gym. I thought he was professional, but he wasn't. He was very, very intelligent. His name was Ryan. He was hard to hit, and he could fight really well. He didn't care what you threw at him, he was ready for whatever came his way. He paid attention to detail and was always being smart about where he was in the ring. As with everything in the world, the man who's the smartest and pays attention to details can be the best.

My first day at Dyme I met a pro boxer named Spidey. He asked me the same question, "How long have you been boxing?"

I told him the same thing I told Smoove. He replied with the same answer, "So did Benard Hopkins. Good job."

I would go to Dyme every day, and then the day came that I finally met Coach Presley who gave me the rundown on the gym. Coach Presley is a very straight forward guy who doesn't leave any room for his words to be miscommunicated or misunderstood. To be the head coach of a boxing gym is something special, you're basically in charge of people who can fight very well, and they respect you.

To be a boxing trainer coach it really means something. It means you actually are what they call an apex predator. You're teaching people how to fight, who can really fight. Coach Pressley was still cool though. Early on I started noticing similarities between him and Magnetic.

From the get go I could tell everything he said he meant. These were the type of qualities that stood out the most to me and that I valued for myself, because that's what made you a man. I would tell people all the time that I was a young man before going to prison, however prison made me a man.

Coach Pressley not only was straightforward and respected, but had a bit of a mean streak. He wasn't the type of person you would want to have as your enemy. I could really respect that. I actually looked up to him because of that. He was very intelligent, and he always knew how to get the best out of people. Just his presence alone would bring the best out of you. He would *command* the best out of you.

During our first conversation he said, "I'm going to let you come in here, you can do some work for me in the gym, workout people in the afternoon, and I'm going to train you at night."

"Cool," I said.

The first time he watches me box, he sees my growth and determination. After a few weeks of skill work and conditioning, I get my first chance to spar. It was definitely a learning experience. It was very severe. I went in there with this one guy named Darius. He weighed a lot less than me, however that didn't mean shit. He had great skills and he was in the ring beating my ass. After a while, you get hit so many times you start thinking, damn I am bleeding, but I'm not knocked out. I started realizing, this is kind of endurable, but I didn't want to hurt, so I did my best to fight back, using the knowledge I learned in prison. He was just overall a better fighter. He knew how to use his feet to his advantage so he wouldn't get hit. He was in a lot better sparring shape than I was. At the end of the day, this is where you notice just how much experience matters.

My next opponent was Ryan, the guy I mentioned earlier. Again, I was doing a few things I learned in prison. We had small sparring or offense to defense drills, so I had some moves I wanted to use, but this was different. I could actually throw punches and fight different styles.

I try to throw punches at Ryan, trying to hit wherever I think I can. None of them were landing, like at all. I started getting a bit cautious, because I noticed he hadn't thrown one punch back yet. Then I threw one lazy jab and he hit me with the hardest punch I've ever had in my life. I froze. I think I was knocked out on my feet. Next thing I know, I hear coach yell, "Stop!

Justin, you got hit because you turned your head. You do that again it might be lights out for you." Then he yelled, "Box!" And we went right back to sparring. He had not one bit of sympathy in his voice, and I appreciated it. That's when I realized what boxing really was, and I loved it.

Granted, it wasn't easy going in there with Ryan or any of the guys who really knew how to box, however the next day someone from another gym came to Dyme for some sparring. We were both on the same level in boxing. He was trained by another coach who boxed professionally. When it was my turn to get into the ring, Coach Presley only said one thing to me, "Go in there and beat his ass."

He was slightly bigger than me and I just remembered doing what I was taught by everyone who trained me. It's amazing how things come together when you are in the moment. The body never forgets. When it's called upon it will respond. Since he was bigger, all I did was move and jab to see how he could move with his feet. He still landed some great punches on me, but overall I felt I did well. Sparring was real, everyone believes wearing head gear cushions the blow, but that's not true. It's only use is to make sure you don't get cut. So every punch was felt.

I left the gym feeling proud of myself that number one, I didn't die, and number two, I had one of the greatest learning experiences of my entire life—that is until I woke up the next morning and my shoulders were on fire. I mean, it was terrible. I remember getting out the bed trying to hold myself up and my arm slipped off the bed. I said to myself, "Alright, this is the real deal, but it was cool. It was real cool."

Boxing started opening my eyes to a different way of seeing life. Not only that, it made me become a different person. It helped me prepare for the road of being home with a record. If I wanted better for myself, then I was going to have to create something better and fight for it every single day.

2014 Reflection

A lot of 2014 was me trying to find my way in the world. In prison, I would write letters from friends, asking them what was going on in the world. I would usually get replies that said something like, you're not missing anything. I knew they were giving me their honest answer, but the reality was I was missing a lot. The world had changed in those three long, but short, years in prison. One way in particular was social media. I mean it was a completely different beast in itself.

Not only did it become such a big business tool, but to me it made everyone the same. Everyone talked the same, posed for pictures the same way, and even wore the same clothes. There were no more regional differences in people. Social media redefined what "local" meant. Everyone was looking to social media as a means of validation.

Another thing that stood out to me was how Google took over the world. Before going to prison, Yahoo was a big thing, however Google destroyed the game entirely. Along with that the cellphone industry had changed dramatically. Before going to prison you had several competing brands: Palm, Nokia, Blackberry, Samsung, and Apple. By 2014 it seemed like it was only Samsung and Apple.

I knew if the world had changed this much, then there were a lot of changes I had yet to even notice. That made me curious as to what was really out there in the world. I also found myself just dwelling in situations I had no business in. Nothing illegal or anything, just certain environments. I was acting like I was trying to relive a life I missed. One thing that guys in the prison talked about was the "prison glow" you have when you get home. They say it's a glow because you look a lot healthier and cleaner than most dudes in the world. No drugs, no alcohol, working out all the time. You start glowing and it was very true.

When I came home, it wasn't one hundred percent quite the experience I thought I was going to have. It took me eight days to have sex when I got home. That had to be the longest eight days of my life. The funny part was I did three years in prison and the time just flew by. I got home, and those eight days were a long stretch.

One of the main things on my mind at the time was getting a job and having sex. The crazy part about that list of priorities was that a lot of people were cool with it. People said things like, "As long as you're staying out of trouble and looking for a job, I know you're going to do your thing."

Before I went to prison, you could shoot your shot to approach women on social media. It didn't work like that when I got home. I noticed a lot of people doing things for clout and attention. That's what seemed to matter at that time in the world: how you looked on social media. Social media dating was a lot to take in. I could see the change happening before going to prison, however being thrown back out in society and having to understand what was taking place was a lot. It was kind of like those movies when a man gets frozen for years, gets unfrozen and then has to understand the world he now lives in. It was too much to process. I also noticed with this big shift in social media a lot of people didn't have confidence in themselves the way portrayed on social media.

The phrase "having it all together" was a big facade. I had a different meaning that wasn't just based on finances but more so based on mentality. In prison, I learned how to look at myself and know myself while it seemed others only focused on their money and never learned the habit of knowing themselves. I had a lot of self confidence. I now had to grow that confidence with money.

By then, most of my college classmates had already graduated. They were to their careers or business. I was in a weird place feeling like I was just getting started but I wasn't. I had desire, I had discipline, I had dedication to the process. I just had to find the right thing to do.

'I Went Back'

I see why a lot of guys locked up would say it was hard to come back home. When I was approaching my release date, people would tell me their stories about going home and coming back to prison. A set of words stood out to me that everyone repeated no matter who was telling their story.

"I went back to doing what I was used to doing," some said. "I went back to hanging with the same people. I went back to my hood," others said. "I went back. I went back. I went back." All of the stories of going back took place, because things got hard financially. Those three words, "I went back" let me know there was a real obstacle I needed to start preparing for when I got home. I didn't know it then, however the obstacle wasn't what was taking place on the outside. The real obstacle was getting rid of bad habits. Habits that hadn't proven to be worth keeping, however out of convenience people would go back to them. Those stories and those three words showed me how determined I truly had to be so as not to resort to something that would cost me my freedom.

Now you're probably thinking, "Justin, how the hell did you get all that out of just three words?"

Orca Moment: In life, listen to the small details in the stories of people

*who made the same decisions that you don't want to make. You can
learn a lot of what not to do from what other people have done.*

After being home a few months, I realized that to make it out in the world, I
was going to have to make some drastic changes. I needed to make some
moves that would put me ahead. I realized what everyone was saying about
it being tough. I went months surviving on the grace of others, however I
wanted to be self-sufficient. I knew I could, it was the how part I was still
figuring out.

Consistent work wasn't easy to find. Everything was only a week or two
and I would be back to square one. While I was doing the job hunt, I was still
actively looking for some type of entrepreneurial endeavors, but everyone I
saw was saturated or wasn't legit as I thought it was, so I had to go back to
the drawing board several times and look for something new.

Finally, after six months back home, I got a call from my cousin Courtney.
He said he had a job for me. It was November 2014 and he just had an open
position. I was ready to take it.

The type of work was retail merchandising. We would be setting up
Advance Auto Parts stores. Sometimes the buildings were just built with
nothing in them and we would have to get the store ready for the grand
opening. My first assignment, however, we were transporting goods back
and forth from an old store to set up a new store. This type of work was
kind of serious. We were out on the road at least eight days and worked
seven days, twelve hours a day. At the end of the day we'd go right back to
our room and get ready to do the same thing over again.

That first assignment, I actually did back-to-back trips. I stayed on the
road for two weeks, and when I finally got paid I was like, wow, this is a nice
little bit of change. I think I got paid somewhere around $1,400. Since my
mother and I didn't have a car, we used that money to rent a car. We would
rent the car on a weekly basis and did that for a while.

After those two trips, there was a dead period. People were getting ready
for the holidays and everything was shutting down. The work with Courtney

was assignment based and if they didn't have any assignments, then there was no work. You had to fend for yourself in the meantime, so I started googling ways to find different lines of work. Nothing really panned out and that was probably a blessing in disguise. The holidays were approaching quickly and it was going to be my first time being with my family for the holidays. That meant a lot to me.

It was good to see all of my family, and I realize how much I missed out on life. I saw my little cousins, Jacob, Lamon, Nicholas and Kennedy. Three years did fly and I really missed that feeling of family. I hadn't seen them in so long. Three years doesn't seem like a long time, until you look at what all took place. Seeing the growth and change in my family was an indicator to me that I'm not here to stand still. I had to start moving and pick up some pieces. The celebration phase was officially over, and it was time to start seeing how I was going to put my life together. I was getting mentally prepared for 2015.

When 2015 arrived, I was still searching for consistent work. and my search led me to find a company named Spar which did retail merchandising in Charlotte and surrounding areas of North Carolina. When I first started, things were going well. I had assignments every week servicing grocery stores, pharmacies, and book stores. I was doing pretty well. The pay was cool, some weeks were better than others. It wasn't life-changing money, but it was consistent. I still didn't like doing all this back-breaking work all day for pay that felt like little to nothing.

I really felt like I was making too much money and logistically I wasn't. It seemed to me that I was just shuffling money around, not really holding on to it. I didn't know what to do with it because I was still in the same cycle or rat race living paycheck to paycheck. It started becoming obvious to me that *making* more money doesn't mean you *have* more money.

In 2015 I had a girlfriend and I started noticing how finances can put a strain on a relationship. There will always be static in your relationship when you are trying to get yourself together but don't know who you fully are. You try to keep your partner happy, but they don't fully know themselves either. I was also learning that neither of us really knew what to do with money or how to change our circumstances and we were taking it out on each other.

* * *

Eventually, I was granted early completion of my post-release program. I didn't have to continuously show up for meetings or have unannounced visits at home. I could party like I wanted to. The day after my completion, I remember getting a hold of the best weed I could find and smoking for the first time in four years. In the moment, it felt good, but at the same time, it wasn't this rewarding feeling I thought it would be. I kept doing it for some time though.

During this time, I noticed I needed some separation, between me and the crowd I was hanging with. It wasn't a negative crowd, but I know I had to start making some kind of separation. I was leaning heavily into phrases like, "your network is your net worth," and "you are the sum of the five people you hang around." I started noticing I wasn't hanging around millionaires or even thousandaires. Most of the people around me were in the same situation I was.

I was still boxing at the gym, however, I didn't really have my head in it too much. I don't know if I was still trying to process the world or process the fact I was so broke. Even before having a girlfriend, I realized the world revolves all around money. No one paid attention to a person if you didn't have money.

I started to notice party scenes, in particular the ones that revolved around college sports. I was working like crazy and my friend Twon and his brother came down for some events. I got to see a little bit of what nightlife was like again. After being out of the loop so long I could tell I wasn't addicted to it like I used to be. It was good to catch up with friends and mingle, but, again, everything revolved around money. That wasn't sitting well with me, not because I didn't have money, but because things can turn out catastrophic if having money was your sole reason for living.

I started to understand the type of life I wanted and started finding ways to attract life. I knew what I didn't want and I tried to fix that by working so much with my cousin Courtney. I would work with him, work on my own and I started noticing I'm trading crazy long hours for money. I didn't feel too good about it and I'm all about manual labor. I saw people get hurt on the job with no insurance, no type of worker's compensation. I saw people get talked to disrespectfully. All the people around me were doing this type of work. We were all in the same boat when it came to finances and employment.

Usually, people were just happy to have income. If you were getting paid, employers could treat you any type of way and you'd be good with it, because it's not like you had many options. When I noticed all this I said to myself, "I'm not with all this."

What I thought was good money, was just an illusion. I saw the writing on the wall and I wanted better. At the same time, I was making money, but I wasn't keeping any of it. It was like I was just making money just to stay in the struggle and have a little bit of fun. I knew I was in a terrible cycle. I was going against my own principles. I was trading in way too much time, and energy for little bits of money. I was shortening my time even more, by smoking weed and drinking.

All of my waking hours I was working, smoking weed, drinking, and being in crazy arguments. Once I started putting the pieces to this puzzle together, I said to myself, "Bruh, I really don't like all of this. This is not what you did three years in prison for just to come home to."

I decided that day to start making some changes. I told myself I was going to have to do some real big boy things to have the life I wanted.

A Better Me

The year that really changed my life was 2015. I was still working with my cousin in Charlotte. I was still stuck in the cycle of not knowing what to do, not knowing what's going on with not only my finances but also my life. To add to it, I found out that my girlfriend was pregnant. I knew I had to start making some real life changes.

The minute I found out she was pregnant was the moment a spark happened. I replayed everything that took place in my life in that doctor's office, and I knew I didn't want my child to go through the same type of things I went through. I didn't know it then, however I was starting the path of what some call breaking generational curses. I knew things had to change, I just needed a starting point, and the easiest place for me to start was health.

Earlier that summer, me and my girlfriend were on a two-week beach vacation when I noticed how much I was eating. I ate so much and partied so much in those two weeks that I lost all my six-pack. I started feeling different and experienced indigestion, heartburn, things I'd never felt before in my life. I thought, "Yo, I have to get back to Dyme ASAP. No matter what, I'm running, I'm getting my body back. Like, this isn't me. This isn't what I want."

We went to the beach Fourth of July weekend, and when I got back to the gym I was so relieved. I was doing well, working out hard, running often.

Looking back at it I could tell I was running toward something else, not just fitness. Something on the inside was taking place as well.

In September, my mom asked if I wanted to go to the Million Man March in Washington DC. I told her I'd go because I liked DC. The Moorish Science Temple had a strong presence in DC. I thought it would be good to do some non-work related travel and be close to other members of the faith I had studied in prison for all those years.

When we got to DC we took the train to capitol hill. When we finally got there it was really one million people in one area. It was a great atmosphere to see all these black people come together for one common cause: liberation. We met up with some of my cousins from DC and Philadelphia. Eventually, the man of the hour, the Honorable Minister Louis Farrakhan, appeared. People had lots of things to say about him. Some were for him and some were against. I never took a definitive stance because I never met him in person, however his words were life changing. That moment made a real impact on my life. I left empowered and confident. That experience amplified my love for myself and what I wanted in life. I was really thankful my mom invited me. Some called him radical or an extremist, however everyone has an opinion. I knew better than to think too much of other's opinions and to go off of what I felt. The message Minister Farrakhan put out there was probably the most powerful thing I've ever heard a black man say out his mouth. I realized that Minister Farrakhan was at the top of his game for a reason.

His words were very real and they came from a place of love and understanding. They were also coming from a place of extreme self-love and love for people. Don't get it confused, I'm not calling him an extremist, however his words were powerful. I once read an article he wrote that said something along the lines of this: When you want to change something in your life, you'll change it. No matter how hard it is, no matter what it is, no matter how impossible it seems. No matter if you die in the process of doing it. That Million Man March left a very profound effect. It woke me up to be a better me.

Orca Moment: The Million Man March made me realize that whatever feelings I had inside my body to be greater, I had to act on. If it doesn't go right, just keep going. If I died doing it, that's alright, but I had to get started doing something.

I left Washington DC knowing I was a different person. I was ready to step into my greatness. After that moment, some relationships had to fall by the wayside. I was about to have a little girl, and I wanted to show her a different level of life. For that to happen, I knew I had to be different too. I would be her visual example of a lifestyle of greatness. I had to display it, and I felt like I wasn't doing that. This is when I knew things were about to get real.

I went home, still went to Dyme and still worked. I would often go to the Charlotte Supplement Store and these Jamaican guys would talk about something called Jamaican wood root tonic. When I asked them about the benefits, they told me it would keep me healthy.

"That's something you need right there," one of them said. "That's something you need right now young man."

I bought the tonic and it tasted terrible, but I could really feel the health benefits they were talking about. I started noticing healthy topics come across my Instagram or Facebook feeds. I ran across information about having a healthy diet and the idea that I was eating dead food that caused people to be sick.

I said to myself, "Dead food, what the hell is that?"

This one post I read was pretty explicit: "Your body is a graveyard. You wonder why there are so many people dying from diseases in the world."

I started to see the point. Eventually, these posts led me to an herbalist named Dr. Sebi. As I did more research, I learned how he cured people of certain diseases. He even cured someone of AIDS using herbs and changing what they ate to a balanced vegan alkaline diet which included no meat, no dairy or high-alkaline foods. After my research, I was really blown away by this man, and he piqued my interest to go vegan.

Transitioning to a vegan diet was hard. I didn't really know what the hell to do. I was going at it on my own. At that time, I was still working with my cousin Courtney, working out, and really just trying to get my head wrapped around re-shaping my life. People were asking me if I was ready to be a dad. Of course I was, however, I was really putting everything together. I never had a plan of action, I was just making moves as they came up.

The next time I went to Atlanta again to work with Courtney, I was really trying to figure this vegan thing out. I thought that maybe I could go vegetarian, or try to incorporate more healthy options. I was straddling the fence and telling myself that I was really doing something, when in actuality I was being indecisive. To me, indecision was worse than anything, but I was doing this because I didn't know what the hell to do.

Orca Moment: Most people dabble or talk themselves out of making big personal changes. Making bold change might not be the popular thing to do, and many people are not dedicated to it. Only a small percentage of people in the world fully dedicate themselves to lasting change, but that's what will put them on the path to success. I didn't want to be like most people and make the same excuses for not committing to change.

One perk of working out of town with Courtney was always working out. Whether it was at the hotel gym or a local gym, all I wanted to do was work out and train. I was absorbing boxing so much, every chance I got I'd go watch something on YouTube on boxing.

Boxing was that thing that kept me going during my lowest times in prison and life. Boxing was the thing that propelled the hell out of me, boxing and running. If you can think in the ring, you're a smart fighter. And if you can see small details, like Coach Pressley, and Coach Smoove, you can excel in life. But first, you have to experience what goes on in the ring. I didn't know it then, but I was training my mind for a bigger fight. I was surrounded by great people—I always wanted to surround myself by great people—and that was key for me. I knew I had to be tactical. I had to be aggressive. I had to turn into something else, and I wanted it so bad.

I was so involved, I would watch Floyd Mayweather on YouTube say, if you want to be a great fighter, you can't smoke, you can't drink, you have to live a clean lifestyle. You have to be dedicated. It's all about being dedicated. Andre Ward would say the same thing. All the top guys, they were living a real clean life, which kept them at the top of their game for as long as possible.

That was what I wanted for myself too. I thought, well if my body really had dead food in it, I wanted a different type of life. I wanted to eat different types of foods.

* * *

I was coming back from Atlanta after another work trip with my cousin. I got into our Greyhound bus and found our seats. Me and this dude were sitting beside each other looking like sardines when this woman said, "Hey, do one of y'all want to move and sit over here? Y'all look kind of cramped over there."

I said yes, and moved to sit beside her. She asked me my name and said her name was Anita. We ended up getting on the topic of football and learned we were both New England Patriots fans. She asked me if I workout and I said I boxed at a gym. I told her I was trying to go vegan. I knew so little about the word that I pronounced it "vay-gan"

"I'm vegan," she said, pronouncing the word correctly.

"Oh shit!" I replied.

Orca Moment: When you put out very strong energy for something you want to happen, little pieces of that thing will start to appear in your life. You've got to gather all these pieces up, whether it's people or education courses. Gather them, pack them up and be ready to ride the gas. Just like the money wave I talked about in prison, these things can come in waves. When momentum picks up in the universe, you have to take it. You have to capitalize on it, because the moment might not come again. It might not be that easy again.

After Anita told me she was vegan, I asked if she would help me out on my journey. She said didn't mind and she would give me pointers and show me some things.

"Who do you listen to the most to learn about veganism?" she asked.

"I like Dr. Sebi," I said. "But what do you suggest?"

"Just go by his list," she said. "If that's who you want to go with, then that's who we're going to go with. Whatever he says, I'm going to help you with it."

One thing I loved about Anita was that even though she was a follower of Dr. Afrikka, she respected Dr. Sebi. She was open to helping me follow him even if he wasn't her particular person.

When I got to Charlotte, I got off that bus so pumped and excited. I went home and told my mom that I could finally go vegan, and that I was really going to do this. I threw out all the food that wasn't vegan. I was ready to go head first. There was nothing else I wanted to do.

This took place in November 2015. I remember the very first time I went to the store fully committed to being vegan. I bought all this food and vegetables. I thought, this is going to be a breeze. I'm not going to have to worry about nothing. I was on the phone with Anita via Snapchat, and after buying the groceries, I got home and asked her, "Now what?"

"Now you have to cut it," she said.

"What?"

"Yes, you have to cut it, you have to prepare it," she said. "You have to do everything."

For a split second I was like, damn do I really have to do all of this?

Orca Moment: When you're thinking of a goal or, getting your dreams, it's easy to never really place together everything that must happen to get to that goal or dream. Most vision boards only have the goal placed on the vision board, and that can leave you discouraged about all the little things that have to take place along the way to that goal. I never really thought about how tedious it would be for me to cook vegan food. I was just thinking how good and healthy it would be to eat. In reality, there was a lot I had to do to have the diet I wanted. Most of the time when you see someone accomplish a goal, you don't see the work that went into achieving that goal. This experience made me realize that every goal I wanted to have, everything I wanted to put in place, there needed to be some precision, some detailed methodical work that would have to take place. That's why you have to enjoy every single step of the way.

When you're after a goal, you just can't believe or buy into thinking, "I did enough. It's not working. Let's go on to something else." *Hell no.* This is a *constant* journey and this helped me fall in love with the process. When you want to do something new, you have to remember there's a "process" to every new thing you do.

I started realizing what the "process" truly was. As I cooked more vegan meals, I realized there weren't too many vegan recipes. Anita told me to group three food items from my food list together, type those items along with the word "recipe" into Google and I'd find something to cook. That turned out to be the easiest way for me to find recipes. After that advice, I cooked anything I could think of and posted my meals everyday on social media. The early stages of me going vegan were very real, but there was a greater transformation taking place.

Of course, everyone around me didn't see the vision like I did and that's cool. Early on, I realized that if I was going to be on this path, then it was going to be all on me. I wasn't going to let up.

Marleigh

Working out in the morning with Coach Smoove is one of the best things that happened to me. It really got me mentally prepared to take on this journey of growth. I was always intrigued by how much ran, sparred and just their overall workout regimen was appealing to me.

One morning I woke up and decided I was going to give the morning crew a shot. I loved working out in the morning anyway, so I figured this would fuel my early-morning workout addiction. The first day we ran probably four miles. I was always a runner, so the run wasn't that bad. After running, we jumped roped, shadow boxed, hit the bag, then got ready to get down to the real business of sparring. I'll never forget we were about to spar and I was a little nervous because I hadn't sparred in a while.

"Don't worry about it," Coach Smoove said. "I'm not going to kill you."

Next thing you know, I hop in the ring and he does the complete opposite of what he just told me. This man *whooped my ass*, I mean real bad, to the point I had to the bathroom to reassess my life. Then I looked at myself in the mirror and I started crying. I said to myself, "We're not going home like this."

I stepped out of the bathroom, walked straight to the ring, and told Smoove I wanted to go another round. I just didn't feel right going home after a performance like that. At that moment, I realized how much I was ready to step up to the challenge that was before me, not just in sparring but in life. I kept my word to myself.

> *Orca Moment: Even when you're not in the best shape, you have to be willing to step up to the plate even when things are hard. No one ever told you getting everything you want was going to be easy. You have to go through the pain, period. Boxing was a great example of how much hell you have to go through to get better. You have to learn how to pay attention to all the small details.*

After I told Smoove I wasn't going home and wanted another round, he looked at me and said, "Alright." This time I fought harder. I still got my ass whooped based, however, I wasn't timid. I knew what to expect and I left the gym with a sense of self-respect. That was the most important thing for me.

Boxing was a metaphor for life. Before I would go to Dyme, I would listen to motivational messages. I would always get my mind prepared for the day. I didn't really know it then but I developed a morning routine. It was so critical that if I didn't stick to my routine, my whole day would be thrown off. If I didn't do my morning meditation, if I didn't go to Dyme, if I didn't spar, if I didn't run, if I didn't work out, everything would be thrown off.

There were times we ran in the cold, in the pouring rain, one hundred degree temperatures, it didn't matter. To be a part of an experience like that every morning made you feel superhuman. It was like nothing the world brought your way would stop you. I was pumped. Every morning I'd go wake up and get ready to take on the world. I still had life going on around me. I had a baby on the way, seasonal work, and me and my future daughter's mother weren't really on the same page about a lot. I was still trying to figure out how my finances would abruptly turn around, however, the gym made life very easy to deal with.

The last few months of 2015, were all about getting ready for the grind. I remember the day Coach Presley told me that I had become good enough to participate in the Golden Gloves tournament. That was cool. I felt I was officially getting better at boxing. I also felt I was getting prepared for parenthood as well.

When 2016 came, I felt it was going to be my year. It was going to be the year everything would just fall into place. I would have a child, live life on my terms and really excel in anything I put my mind to. However, I had a very basic way of thinking. Believing things would just "fall into place" is almost the same level as fairy tales or imagination. There's no plan, only a dream.

I was still on my vegan journey and training for my first fight. I'd been going hard for months, and the days leading up to the fight I was kind of nervous, but everyone had those first-fight jitters.

I ended up losing my first Golden Gloves fight. As I look back on it now I realize several reasons why I lost. None of these reasons had to do with my boxing ability, but when you're on the stage, the pace picks up. The guy wasn't even hitting that hard, but I lost confidence in my abilities. The other fighter was very awkward, and I didn't have a lot of time to figure him out. That in itself was frustrating, and all of that comes into play when you're fighting. He had weird angles and movements, none of which I had seen in the gym before. I wanted to stick to my fight plan as much as possible.

My breathing was crazy. I had never been trained how to breathe properly. I thought to myself, why am I so tired already? What the hell is going on? I was doing too much thinking, and when I lost, I felt like everything I trained for was for nothing.

In boxing, no one likes losing. Floyd Mayweather set the bar so damn high that people wanted to go undefeated their entire career. When I lost that fight, I really felt defeated. I didn't want to give up on life. I didn't want to give up on boxing, but I just felt defeated and hurt. After that loss, I felt it was going to be a very rough year. The Golden Gloves was in February. I was hoping to get things back going on some type of path of normalcy, but by March I received some more devastating news.

I got a text from my best friend Shelton, letting me know his dad, who I called Uncle Al, had died suddenly. Uncle Al was like a father to me. He treated me like he did his own child since I was a boy. Lt. Colonel Allison Dean Hall served twenty-eight years in the Air Force, and he was easily one of the greatest men I had the pleasure to share time with. He always did his best to keep a smile on his face. Uncle Al's death hit me harder than I had imagined. Before he passed, he asked me how I felt about becoming a dad. I told him I was up to the challenge and he said he was eager to meet my daughter. When he died, I realized that would never happen now. That shit hurt bad.

Two weeks later I had a dream about my own dad which was strange because my dad and I didn't have a great relationship. The last time I had seen my dad was when I was thirteen years old in eighth grade. I don't remember much about this dream. I do remember him trying to give me advice on something and I said, "Man, whatever."

"Who the fuck you think you talking to?" he replied.

Even in a dream that felt entirely too real. I was twenty-six at the time and thought I was going to be punished or something *in my dream*. Then I received a phone call that woke me up out of my sleep. I answered the phone. It was my brother Lou who told me my dad had just died. I was barely awake and this was the first call I got. It shook the hell out of me.

I started recognizing what vibrations really were. It felt like the unseen parts of life were becoming clear.

The death of my dad was really tearing me up, because the last conversation I had with him was when I was in college. He called me, I asked who it was and when he said it was him, and I hung up. Thinking back, I think I was being controlled by society to really hate him, and after his death I realized something.

Orca Moment: I could not love my full self without loving my dad. No matter what took place I realized I couldn't talk shit about the man who gave me the ability to talk shit. As a kid, I used to do what was popular, you know, black boy talking shit about his dad and people in society would somewhat agree with me. But even if my dad did 999 things incorrect, the one thing he did correct was be in the correct place and correct time to create me. That alone deserves respect.

Even though my dad was eighty-eight years old when he passed, when you lose a parent something changes in you. Something changed in me for the better. I understood a new level of love. I understood the love I wanted to give to my own child. I wanted to give my daughter, Marleigh, the type of love I felt I didn't get from my dad. My dad and I never had those father-son bonding moments nor did we have a strong relationship.

I was going through a lot of turmoil in 2016. To add to that, I didn't have the most solid relationship with Marleigh's mom. A lot of things were falling apart. I lost the mental focus I needed to keep boxing. Someone suggested that I needed to stop for a while. In hindsight, I wish I hadn't listened to that advice but I did.

I started going through this panic-hustle mode. I call it that because I was doing a lot of hard work, but I wasn't doing anything with the funds. I hated that cycle about myself. I started thinking about what I wanted as my legacy and how I would build it. I didn't know how.

After Uncle Al and my dad died, the only thing I had to look forward to was my daughter Marleigh's birth. I took her mom to the doctor on a Tuesday when they noticed something unusual. Her blood pressure was kind of high, on the verge of preeclampsia. They needed to get the baby out fast so they induced her into labor.

We ended up staying in the hospital for two days. I didn't know what to expect, but in that hospital room, when I saw Marleigh born, I recognized everything I had done within the last year that led to this one moment of me becoming a great father.

Fatherhood was something I knew I was not going to fail at. The minute she was born, things changed. I didn't want to be stuck in this debt trap for much longer. Marleigh's mom and I were going through some very rough battles which ended with us going to court and experiencing some dark times. I knew I had to do something groundbreaking. I knew it was possible to get out of my situation, however it would take something legendary to turn things around. All the great people dedicate themselves to the process of being legendary. I was up for the challenge, because I knew all I had to have was the willpower to continue learning. That was powerful in itself.

After Marleigh was born, there would be many times I'd watch her during the day until her mom got off of work. Several times it was just Marleigh and me all day at the house. I accepted this position because it allowed me access to my daughter all day and gave me the opportunity to create the life I wanted for us. Those were the two most important things: time with Marleigh and time to create.

One sunny day I was holding Marleigh and walking around the cul-de-sac at my mom's house where we lived. I said to myself, "I don't know what's going on in the world, but something great is going on right now. If I get there early and learn and take advantage, I can change my life forever."

I didn't know what that was, but I knew I always had an eye for greatness, for the next big thing. It was a talent of mine. I remember in 2011 while I was still in prison I was reading the USA Today Money Section. I read about the Tesla space program and remembered hearing that NASA was ending its space program. I wrote to my mom saying she should buy Tesla stock. She never did and when I got home Tesla was taking over the world. I felt I was too late, however I knew I needed to rely on this instinct of mine. It's the same instinct I'd been referring to through the duration of this book, I had to step into an apex predator mentality. I've always had this eye for greatness, whether it was great people, great scenarios or great conditions. I started looking at things like how I would in prison. I needed to take advantage of every single thing around me to change my outcome, because the path I was on was a trap that I was not willing to participate in any longer.

50 Cent

I started looking up to certain people who impacted business and changed their life in a way that was similar to mine. The first person who came to mind for me was one of my favorite businessmen who also happened to be a good rapper. I'm not gonna say he was my favorite rapper, but he definitely made a mega impact in a way that was respected. That man was Curtis James Jackson, better known as "50 Cent."

Most people probably see 50 Cent as this big asshole shit talker, who's known for putting Ja Rule's career to bed. However, what I noticed about 50 Cent was something very different. He self-proclaimed his success and manifested the life he wanted when he came home from prison. 50 Cent is one of the greatest prison stories ever in my eyes and that's what I admired about him. His debut album was called "Get Rich Or Die Trying" and getting rich is just what he did.

Just the title of the album was his way of saying he was putting it all out on the line and whatever happens happens. As a black man facing the adversity we face on a regular basis, it was very powerful to even witness how he did it.

The majority of black people commit crime because of poverty, and the getting rich or die trying mentality is already in most of us. 50 Cent just made it to an album. He was never really a rapper, though, he was always a businessman. That's one of the greatest things about him. I felt I could identify with his story. I just had to find a way to get into the door of entrepreneurship in a way that would work.

I follow the brash behavior of 50 Cent, but his mindset was unbelievable. 50 Cent had the confidence and that as long as he got in the industry, he was going to do whatever he felt like doing. It's like my uncle Bobby used to say: "Jay, as long as you have money, everything will work out. As long as you have the mind and the money you can make whatever you want happen."

One of 50 Cent's songs called "Hustlers Ambition" he says:

"I want the finer things in my life

So I hustle.

Nigga you get in the way while I'm trying to get mine

And I'll buck you.

I don't care who you run with, or where you from

Nigga fuck you

I want the finer things in my life,

So I hustle."

50 Cent hit the rap scene around 2002. He made this particular song in 2005, after he came home from prison. That lets you know what was on his mind the entire time he was coming up. I knew that was the same mentality I had to embody coming home from prison as well. I was looking for ways to save my life. That was my state of mind in 2016. I knew I had to do something truly groundbreaking.

I didn't know how to get started, I just knew I had to get the ball rolling on something. Then, one of my friends tasted my vegan cooking and suggested I sell vegan food. That's exactly what I decided to do. I contacted my friend Ryan to create a logo, and I came up with the name Vegan On The Go. I had four items: a power bowl, fajitas, burrito and spaghetti. To be completely honest, I didn't know what the hell I was doing, however I was doing something and that's what mattered to me.

Cooking food was a process I wasn't ready for, however I embraced the challenge. I told people they could place an order twenty-four hours in advance to give me time to cook and deliver the food to them. I was one of the first—if not the very first—to deliver cooked vegan food to people's homes.

Doing Vegan On The Go opened doors for me in the vegan community. It wasn't where my passion really was, but it got my mind going in the correct direction.

As I started building this business for myself, Marleigh's mother and I were still at odds. I was still strapped for money and Vegan On The Go wasn't something I saw myself doing long term. I had to trade too much time for money, and it wasn't even my passion. I remember holding Marleigh, walking around the cul-de-sac at my mom's place saying, "Something is going on in the world that is so powerful. If I'm there early enough I can take advantage of it and really be ahead of the curve."

I knew that being "early" was the missing link to real wealth. I needed to find something life changing for me to turn my situation around. It's funny how manifestation works because soon after, in July 2016, I found my breakthrough.

Bitcoin

Honestly, I can write an entire book about Bitcoin. Right now, however, you will learn how this was the ultimate game changer. If you know me or have followed me on social media for a while before purchasing this book, then you know the amount of blood sweat and tears I put in with Bitcoin.

Throughout the rest of this book, you will learn Bitcoin tricks and strategies I used to be successful. If you really want to take a deep dive into Bitcoin—which I highly recommend you do—send me an email at justin@bitcoinvegan.com saying, "I need to learn Bitcoin correctly."

I look forward to hearing from you.

The Ultimate Game Changer

One day my mom told me about this investment platform run by a company called Coince. I had never heard of it, and when I went on their website, I just saw the bitcoin symbol. I remember seeing it on the movie *Dope* so I thought, let's see what this is about. It was called an investment platform. You send money, and it'll give you a payout after a certain number of days, so I figured I'd give it a try.

I remembered my friend Isaiah Jackson, who I ran into in 2015. The reason his name popped into my head was because his Instagram name was BitcoinZay. Instantly, I started putting the pieces to the puzzle together. Long story short, that investment platform my mom told me about turned out to be some type of elaborate scam. However, I knew Zay, and I knew he wasn't a scammer, so there had to be some legitimacy to this. I decided to reach out to him about Bitcoin. When I called, he sounded so happy to share his knowledge with me—at least what I could handle at the moment.

"It's a decentralized currency," Zay said. "Meaning it's not controlled by governments or banks. It's a storage of value similar to gold but better. You can use it like money and spend it anywhere in the world that you please. It's something that could change the world, and it could change your life. It's not a get-rich-quick scheme, but if you do it correctly, you stay patient and have the proper knowledge, it can change everything for you."

When Zay mentioned the benefits of Bitcoin, I was instantly all the way in. It seemed so radical at the time. I had to give it a try and know for sure if it was legit. I really didn't know what to do with myself. This was during a time in my life when I knew I had to play a longer game with Bitcoin.

"If I keep bitcoin and hold on to it," I asked. "Would I be able to buy a house with this?"

"You could do whatever you want with it," Zay said. "As long as you keep acquiring knowledge and you stay patient, you can do whatever you want."

After that conversation, I started researching everything I could find on Bitcoin. I started noticing just how many people were against it, and that only added more fuel to my fire. I've always noticed how the majority of people will always follow the same trend, and if I wanted to make a quantum leap toward my goals, I had to go on the path less traveled.

During my research, I stumbled across some graphs showing bitcoin's growth potential. I noticed how it would always appreciate over time. I saw it had some serious dips and I thought, OK that gives it legitimacy. This is something real. If it was a linear line going up, I would be skeptical.

Once I noticed what the graphs said, and I was cool with that. The little legitimate research I could find only fueled my desire to move forward. I also considered the opposite of what people were saying. Some were saying, bitcoin is kind of scary or governments don't trust it. That's when I knew this is exactly where I should be.

That's when it all started. I would call Zay probably more times than anyone in the world. I was on YouTube almost every day. These were some of the golden days of Bitcoin.

When I learned about Bitcoin from Zay, I hadn't done any vegan cooking for a while. I didn't have much money. I was still working retail jobs, but the first time I got paid, the first thing I did was buy bitcoin. It was July 9, 2016 when I bought my first piece of bitcoin. Back then the price of bitcoin was around $650 to $700. I knew I could save up that much money to get a whole bitcoin, but I never really understood what I was doing. I just knew I had to be a part of this. I *had* to be in this.

I remember my mom would tell me how my granddaddy had a great eye for certain stocks, certain companies. I was like, well he had his great moments. This is going to be *my* great moment for *my* family. I knew I was going to make it work. No matter the cost, this was going to work.

Now that I was committed to bitcoin, another beast I needed to tackle was social media. Social media was a big deal, and I was trying to find ways to take advantage. I was coming to a point in my life when I could tell I was about to be in between jobs. I was making some good money, the best money I had made in my life at that time, but I could tell it was about to come to an end.

Now that I had bitcoin, I felt I had a new purpose with my Vegan On The Go. I remember Zay saying I could use bitcoin as a payment system, so I hit him up and asked him if I could accept bitcoin for my business.

"Hell yeah!" he said.

"Cool," I said.

I kept the same menu as before, but this time I added a QR code for bitcoin to let people know I accepted it as payment. Everything I was doing, I was doing with zero experience, from running a business to buying bitcoin as an investment. I had taken the Dr. Sebi approach to things. The approach was simple: You *get* in the field and *learn* in the field. None of this was easy by any means, however the most important thing I had to do was get in there.

Orca Moment: *If you ever desire to be great at anything, you just have to get in there. Again, you have to get in there.*

I knew nothing about selling food, however a friend of mine sold food stamps. I would buy the food stamps, buy the food, cook the food and sell it for a profit. I treated it like a hustle. Like selling weed or selling stuff in prison. I didn't know any other way to get started, other than rely on my previous knowledge.

I'm pretty positive I didn't really make any money outside of just shuffling money around and paying for gas, but I learned a lot. I can't say this whole experience was for nothing. I learned what inventory was. I learned how to work a system. It awakened something in me that had lain dormant for a long time—the drive to be my own boss, to hustle, to meet the challenge of creating a business.

When I officially published my flyer with the bitcoin QR code, it started to look like something next level. A vegan food delivery service that accepts bitcoin? I was just elated.

The first thing I started doing was making connections with people. I wasn't into networking, because I really didn't know what the hell to do, however my mom told me about a group called the Fuller and Dudley Mastermind Group. They would have meetings every Monday for entrepreneurs and I would just go there and try to soak up as much business knowledge as possible.

One thing I noticed early on about entrepreneurship is that you need to understand who you choose to go into business with. I met a lot of people who knew about street hustling but didn't know too much about making things mutually beneficial for themselves and their clients. Most people had a shark mentality instead of an orca mentality. Most didn't look at business as a way for everyone to advance. It was just me, me, me. I also noticed how people loved to take advantage of upcoming entrepreneurs saying things like, "Oh, you got a great entrepreneurial spirit, you should come work for me."

Some people would take that easy route out which is exactly what I did one time. I'm not going to name the man or his company, but things started off cool. I met a businessman who offered me to work for him while I ran my own business. I thought what he offered sounded pretty cool and could put a little extra money in my pocket. Nope. I should have listened to my mom about this guy when she said, "Justin, he's looking for an employee."

I said, "He seems to be pretty cool. It'll be alright."

She looked at me with a face that said, yeah ok whatever.

The man told me we would have these calls every morning around 6 a.m. I soon realized most of these calls just dealt with him talking junk about everybody's business. I never intended to start my mornings off like that.

Part of me thought, well, let's see what's on the other side of this. There may actually be some good that comes out of this situation. The first assignment was so simple. It paid $100 plus he would buy the food I was selling. But if I could, I would refund all the money I ever earned from him.

The man had a product from another century. He offered me a job based on the premise that I could still work my business and make money on the side with him. It turned out he was really trying to pull me away from my business and take on his full time. I soon realized working for him was a big waste of time. I had to cold-call people who weren't interested in an outdated product. I remembered something I read in *The 48 Laws of Power* about always staying current with the times. You don't want to just be doing things that seem cool. Make yourself relevant for the times.

A big lesson I learned early was to stay the course with your business. Be careful who you network with and don't just work with people because they are offering you money while your business takes off. That approach will ultimately turn you away from what you want to achieve.

Your situation can be whatever you make it. Early on I came to that realization. I was getting denied from all these jobs, yet I was bringing in enough income to stay where we were living and stay alive. Marleigh was cared for by both my family and her mother's family. I had some type of support and that gave me time to put a plan together that would change my life.

One of the greatest things I realized was this: If you know what your dream is, and you are going to make it happen, don't shortchange yourself by taking your eye off the ball when things get hard. Don't deviate from the plan just because things get scary. That's exactly when you have to lean in. I learned not to shortchange my dreams. I was committed to the plan. I learned wealth comes with time and knowledge—not just more money.

When I discovered bitcoin, I knew things were falling into place the way I wanted, but it was only the beginning.

Vegan Coaching

D oing Vegan On The Go was always some type of learning experience in the world of entrepreneurship. As I mentioned before with Dr. Sebi, this whole thing was about jumping in the field and seeing what you can create. Seeing what you can stir up and what information you can gather along the way.

I learned that the food industry is very complex. It just wasn't something you just did without passion. Cooking was a mixture of attitude plus hunger. At that time, I had to educate a lot of people about veganism. I created Vegan On The Go with the goal of sharing healthier eating options in the black community. No matter where you are—except for probably Atlanta—most black communities only have fast food options. The lack of healthy options plays a major role in your quality of life. That was a whole lecture in itself and it was something I didn't feel like doing. I felt being an educator was taking too much time.

As I mentioned my whole concept was giving black people healthier eating options, but that was just my dream. I realized there was a lot more to this than just cooking food and delivering it. When I started doing Vegan On The Go in November 2016, I was so amped about it. Donald Trump had just been elected president, and I felt that was a spark that made me go into the direction of entrepreneurship. Most people feared the energy that came along with Trump becoming president. I, on the other hand, embraced it.

By the looks of his campaign, Trump wasn't giving out any assistance except to who he chose, and his election fueled me to go even harder with being an entrepreneur. I was ready for any type of hell he caused.

When 2017 came, I really lost all the spark I had with Vegan On The Go. I still wanted to be an entrepreneur, but I had the last straw with cooking. A local womens' group reached out to me and asked if I could cook two dishes for one hundred people at their event—about two hundred meals. I remember going home and being in the kitchen for hours. I made everything by hand, my spaghetti noodles, my pita bread, everything. I worked non-stop for like five hours in the kitchen and I can literally say I destroyed that kitchen.

Once I got to the event, I learned they already had food. I looked back at my text messages and realized they asked me to be a vendor—they weren't asking to pay me. Immediately, some people liked my food, but vegan food was not the majority of the people's preference that evening.

That was the day I said to myself, this is a lesson. I'm just going to have to put this one to the side. I knew cooking was not my thing. I didn't like the lessons or the time that came with it. I had to sit and be honest with myself and realize that cooking food was not going to bring me the life I wanted. It was time consuming and I wasn't willing to put that much time in cooking.

During my whole vegan-cooking experience, people would always say to me, "I want to go vegan, can you help me go vegan?"

I said, "Sure, I can be your vegan coach."

And that's exactly what I did. I thought to myself, hell, I know enough—I'm vegan. I did this and I'm pretty good. I could teach people how to do this too. Ironically, when I made a decision to do this, I got a call from a friend of mine, Mr. Lawrence Wingate. He told me he had a person to refer to me who wanted to talk about veganism. I was shocked like hell how fast this all came into reality. I told him to give her my information. Soon after, her friend called me.

"Yeah, my girl is going to hit you up," she said. "She wants to go vegan."

"OK," I said. "I can help."

She gave me her email, and that was the first time I got to coach someone through a referral. I didn't pay too much attention to how it went down, however, in hindsight, that part was key. I emailed and asked if she would mind having a conversation with me about what she wanted. If she liked our conversation, I would work with her for one hundred dollars a month. She accepted, and we had a brief conversation. She said she would be at VegFest Jr, a plant-based food festival, and we could also meet there.

When I finally got there and walked around, I gave her a call. She said she was walking in the door. I was immediately blown away with how fine she was. I didn't know it at the time, but Tiarra Monreal would soon become my girlfriend.

Tiarra ended up becoming my very first vegan client. I was hyped, because I felt like I was officially a vegan coach. She told me she'd gone months without eating meat, but just couldn't stop eating cheese. I told her the most common thing new vegans go through is trying to find a replacement food for their old diet. I told her that it wouldn't take long to get her off cheese.

One of the things I struggled with early on was figuring out how to get the word out about me being a vegan coach. I tried posting online. I wanted to use social media to the fullest. At that time I was just following what I saw everybody else do: make crazy posts and goofy videos, but I didn't really know there was a professional way to do social media. I knew that social media was going to be the way for me to get ahead. I liked it because it didn't seem to have many overseers. You could use your creativity and use it to network or meet people. Coming home from prison, social media seemed like a cheat code I needed to use.

One day on Instagram, this guy hopped in my inbox and said he could help me get leads online. I was curious to see what he could do. I remember someone once saying that as an entrepreneur you don't want to have to do all the work. You need to delegate your tasks to others, because you can't know how to do everything.

One thing I know I didn't know was marketing. I asked him exactly what he did. He said, "We find you leads from various hashtags. We comb out who your target audience is and how they will see your post. Basically we find your target client."

I told him, cool. I wanted to see what that would be like. I made the investment and gave it a shot. I'm sharing this experience because I realize I should have stayed in communication with this guy. I was so surprised by how many people actually just started hitting me up and wanted to know more about my business.

I noticed an increase in followers almost instantly. They were liking all the material I was putting out about being a vegan coach. I'm thinking, like, damn this cool. It really blew my mind. When Tiarra first became my client I was charging one hundred dollars a month. After noticing the type of people coming to me, I knew I had to raise my price. I changed it to one hundred and fifty dollars a month. (Yeah, I know that's a big difference).

After a few posts and conversations with people who liked my material, I ended up getting four new clients who all paid one hundred and fifty dollars a month. Three of them lived in the Charlotte area and one was in Ohio. So within one week I made six hundred dollars. I said, "OK, that's cool. I can do this."

This is when my coaching career really started. Needless to say I wasn't very good at vegan coaching. Becoming a vegan was bigger than just diet change—it was a lifestyle change.

I couldn't charge my girlfriend anymore, and the few other people I had just ended up falling by the wayside, except for this one woman in Ohio named Mila. She actually taught me that there was more to coaching than just pointing my finger saying, "You need to do this. You need to eat like this."

She was the person who made me realize most people change their diet because of a lifestyle change—not the other way around. The same was true for me. I knew I needed to tap into how to become a more effective coach and rather than just talking about food.

2017

C oaching is a very intense way of living. You have to really understand human psychology—something I didn't know how to do. On top of that, 2017 was a very rough year. I recall times I got paid like one hundred and fifty dollars a month and sometimes even less.

Orca Moment: I knew this wasn't where I was always going to be, but I had to find a way to dedicate myself to one thing. I had to find a way to move forward.

Luckily, the bitcoin I had saved up over time was rapidly rising in price. I was able to take care of some expenses with bitcoin I'd earned in 2016. This was very useful, but I knew I was going against the purpose of Bitcoin. I knew I was missing something because I shouldn't have to use this bitcoin so early. I would get frustrated. I felt like I was betraying myself. If I wanted my bitcoin to work the way it should, I needed to do something totally different. This caused a bit of turmoil in the beginning, especially in my relationship with Tiarra. I was down, but I wasn't out. I felt I didn't know anything about business, but I told myself I had to stay the course. This was only part of the process. I always remembered some of the stories of the celebrities I respected like Kobe Bryant, Floyd Mayweather, Tyler Perry, 50 Cent, even Gucci Mane.

Each of them had a unique drive to keep going no matter what. I always reminded myself, this was a part of the process to reach greatness. It's what you go through to become legendary. I wanted to do something legendary with my life and what I learned along the way would get me there.

Some months it got so bad I don't even remember how I made it through. I wasn't doing Vegan On The Go, I wasn't doing merchandising, and I only had a few jobs that paid consistently.

My only source of income were these online bitcoin consultations I offered sporadically. At this point, I was fully submerging myself in Bitcoin. I was even selling bitcoin to people in the streets. I knew where all the bitcoin ATMs were located (more on that to come), and I would go and buy bitcoin for people at a premium before it was banned by the FBI.

Around this time I was learning deeply from one of my Moor brothers with the Moorish Science Temple of America. His name was Miller-El, owner of Murex Bitcoin Solutions.

I was introduced to him by a mutual Facebook friend. All we did was immerse ourselves in learning the power of Bitcoin. Miller-El and his co-founder, Free Bey, were some of the greatest coaches I had in this space. While I was financially broke at the time, I was studying what the financial future of the world might hold.

Aside from learning Bitcoin, I was a victim of shiny object syndrome. I wasn't really committed to doing one thing, because every passing thing caught my attention. When something wasn't moving fast enough, I'd jump on to the next thing. If I wanted to go deep ahead, I had to do something that was going to make my next move my best move.

Coaching was cool. I actually liked coaching. I was always meeting new people online and I found myself always in a sales mode. I didn't know how to sell, however what I did know was how to present myself. I heard someone say, as long as you fail forward you are headed in the correct direction.

Much of 2017 was a blur of hope. I was starting to feel the effects of coming home from prison, being short on cash and not having many job options. What helped me tremendously was focusing on being a father to Marleigh. I based all my decisions on how I wanted to build a better foundation for her future.

But even with this perspective, things were rough. Everything I thought was going to happen in 2016 didn't, and I was in a mental funk for all of 2017. I reached a great epiphany and realized I needed to turn the ship around. I didn't know how or even why I felt stuck, but I knew the answer would be revealed very quickly.

I'm happy to say I don't remember most of 2017. That was the year I spent planning what it would take to have a thriving future. I wanted the next year to be all about clairvoyance and synchronicity. This meant I would take the signs I felt the universe was giving me and I would run with them. I always had an eye for spotting greatness. Now it was time to lean into 2018. I wanted to stop questioning and just start living without restraints or guilt.

Throughout all of 2017, I was frequently posting about Bitcoin on Facebook and Instagram. Some people told me I didn't know what I was doing and shouldn't be talking about Bitcoin. I was so into it and thinking so much about the future I didn't care. I knew there would be a day that Bitcoin couldn't be ignored anymore. I kept pushing the issue to share information and educate.

Midway through the year, Zay shared with me that he would be moving to Los Angeles and starting a YouTube show on cryptocurrency. He'd run it with an old friend called The Gentlemen Of Crypto. They planned to go live daily spreading news and busting myths on Bitcoin and cryptocurrency. He told me he would need my help for the show and asked me to research as many altcoins as possible before the show went live. In exchange, he would pay me one hundred dollars a week in bitcoin.

Researching all those coins definitely took some time; however, I learned a lot about the crypto industry as a whole. I quickly found out why buying bitcoin was an overall better option than really buying anything on the face of the planet—outside of investing in yourself. Everything else was a depreciating asset. Compared to bitcoin, it all seemed worthless, which is why for the greater part of 2017 I threw myself head-first into Bitcoin.

Orca Moment: The reason I knew Bitcoin would explode is because it's an entirely new financial system that included everyone—not just a select few. What stood out to me the most was there weren't many black people in the space. I knew this was key: for anything to catch fire, black people needed to be involved. I wanted to be the go-to Bitcoin expert. I also knew getting involved early in technology really pays off. Getting people to understand this was important. I was focused on knowing where the world was headed, not where it had already been.

Around the end of 2017 bitcoin was going crazy. Very, very, very, very, very, crazy. It was valued at all-time highs around $18-19,000. Bitcoin gave me the opportunity to support myself a bit while I wasn't working or earning that much. During my early introduction to Bitcoin, I wasn't using it as a long-term investment; I was using it to take care of myself. That's just one of the many benefits of this currency. While most people were skeptical of Bitcoin, or downright never even heard of it, I was already living off of this technology. That itself is amazing.

When I first bought bitcoin, it cost around $600 to $700. Now that it was taking off, I felt a bit relieved. I noticed how being an early adopter of something relatively unknown was working out for me. I started Vegan On the Go to not only take care of my everyday needs but also to buy bitcoin.

All the other little jobs I did were to buy bitcoin. A great friend of mine named Jimmy had a lawn care service. At one point, I hit him up and said, "Jimmy I need some work badly. Whatever you have for me to do, I can do. I just need some work so bad."

"Don't worry I got you," he said. "The most I can give you is ten dollars an hour. I can't guarantee I'm going to always have work, but when I do I'm always going to have your back."

Jimmy was a real good friend simply because he gave me a shot. I remember one time we were driving and talking. He was telling me how he'd been working, saving money, and investing his money ever since he left college. I told him how I would feel depressed because I was financially down and out.

"Justin, you are comparing yourself to everyone else," Jimmy said. "You forget the fact that you went to prison for three years. So from the age of twenty-one to twenty-four, when everybody else is getting their stuff in order with their finances, you were in prison. You gonna make it, Justin. It might not look like it now, but you will make it."

I will always be grateful for Jimmy, because those were some rough times for me. His words and actions were enough to get me by, even if it was only for a little bit.

Back in those days, when people talked about their investments I would feel small. My focus was blinded by material riches—not real wealth. At times, I would forget I had bitcoin stowed away for a rainy day. However, starting with zero dollars and no real income, made it hard to HODL (a term used in Bitcoin meaning Hold On for Dear Life). I had to remember, however, I had the greatest investment of all—time.

In late December, I remember receiving a message from someone on Instagram asking me to be on their podcast show to talk about Bitcoin. Around that time bitcoins were about $11,000 a coin. I agreed to go on the show and make my first podcast appearance. The name of the show was *The Front Porch NC*. The hosts were called Tah and Jason, two West Charlotte High School alumni.

I was forever grateful for this opportunity. It gave me publicity, it gave me some notoriety and the feeling that people actually wanted to talk to me about Bitcoin. The interview helped a lot of people open their eyes to what Bitcoin was. Even my homeboy Vonte said, "Bruh. I finally get it! I finally get what you've been talking about this entire time." Vonte telling me he finally understood something about Bitcoin was one of the best things that came out of that interview.

One of the main things I focused on was investing in my future. I realized I was trying to get money for right now. I had hopes of making it big, but

I kept falling short because I didn't have any long-term plan for earning money. When I met with Miller-El he would preach the value of having skills to succeed in today's world. If you don't have any skills for the era, you will eventually be pushed out.

Before the end of 2017 bitcoin reaches values between $18,000-$19,000.

I said to myself, "What the fuck?"

2018

I didn't tell anyone for awhile that I had this money. I can honestly say now I didn't know what to do with it, so I did what a lot of young people do when they receive an influx of money: travel, have some fun and, for lack of a better way to put it, piss it off. I remember the first time I told my mom and Tiarra how much I was holding they were shocked. I mean *shocked*. One of the reasons I told them was because I wanted to make more renovations to the house.

Then, around January or early February, the price of bitcoin started tanking *badly*. This happened for many reasons, however, one particular reason was how long it took to finalize a bitcoin transaction. Normal people thought it was crazy to have to wait ten minutes for a transaction to finalize. Within the actual banking system it takes weeks for a transaction to really show on their account. This thought pattern is what let me know we still had a long way to go for people to understand the real power of bitcoin. People still loved their Visa transactions better. Most people at the time were buying bitcoin based off of hype. Before this dip in 2018, the price was going up and up. Some people, however, bought their bitcoin too late. They bought it at its peak price, just before it began to tank. When that happened, they started cashing out. Bitcoin then took forever to send because the network was crowded with people. Some were just using it for trading purposes, some were trying to buy up cheap bitcoin and the price of the coin continued going down.

> **Orca Moment:** *Most people believed this meant bitcoin was broken, and it wasn't useful not remembering how the internet evolved from needing a phone connection to WiFi. Bitcoin wasn't any different. That's one of the other side effects of Bitcoin. Once you take your money to this level of freedom, everything opens up as well.*

I still had some good money in Bitcoin, so I was good, according to the life I was living at that moment. I knew moving forward, however, I needed a real plan, because it felt like I was back to square one. I still wanted to do coaching, but I just didn't know how to crack that nut. That was really a thorn in my side. I knew creating a life on my own terms came with walls I had to break down, however this wall here was like steel.

I remember being at Bean Vegan restaurant (this is me paying attention to the signs of synchronicity) when I saw someone come in the restaurant with a DoorDash bag. I asked what they did, and the guy told me they picked up and delivered food.

I told Tiarra at that moment I was going to apply for DoorDash. She said, go for it. What stood out to me was I could make money and still have control over my time. It was perfect for me. I went to the DoorDash headquarters in Charlotte to apply and sit for an orientation. They did on-site background checks, and even though I was confident I could get the job I was still nervous. I had a lot of anxiety about filling out job applications and waiting on background checks to clear.

After about an hour wait, the woman came out and said, "Alright, Justin, you're hired." I jumped up and down with joy.

"What the hell," she said. "What happened? What's up?"

"I have a felony on my record," I said. "This is the first time I passed a background check."

"I'm very happy for you," she said.

This was the start to my DoorDash career. Things started off cool at first, driving around picking up food; however, I quickly noticed how taxing delivering food can be on your mind, body, and your car. I don't advise anybody doing this as a full-time job, but when you need funds, you have to do what you have to do. It seemed cool enough to make the money and be able to use it when you need to, however living off deliveries is not ideal. I remember going out driving at least three times a day.

I slowly started realizing I was in the same trap as I was with Vegan On The Go. I was using a lot of my energy and time for small pieces of money.

One day I was out delivering with Tiarra. I told her, "I need to find me a career, or something to create a career out of. I think I really want to be a coach."

After that I went to Google and searched how to become a health coach. I said to myself, the first thing that pops up, I'm going with it. The first thing I saw on Google was a company called The Health Coach Institute. I clicked on their link. The website seemed cool. I noticed there were a lot of white women, but that was cool. What really stood out was they listed these four pillars you would have to go through to become certified.

Pillar One was centered around your own personal health and your clients' health. Pillar Two focused on how to deliver a twelve-week coaching session to a client. Pillar Three was about how to close a deal and deliver a sales process. Pillar Four focused on how to build your business.

After reading this I was like, wow. What stood out to me the most was the coaching process and building a business. I said to myself, I can do this. Next, I called them up for the very first time, and a woman named Katie answered the phone. We got to talking for a while when I made my decision.

"I think I really want to do this," I told her. "I tried to be a coach on my own and it really didn't get me anywhere."

"Well, Justin, let's give it a shot," she said.

She broke down the prices, and said I could do six payments at $800 or twelve payments of $600. While she was running through the prices I started thinking, how the hell am I going to pull this together strictly from DoorDashing?

A few weeks later I received a call back from HCI.

"I want to do this," I told them. "I'm going to take a chance."

This time, I was asked to come up with only $200 a month to start. I signed up and officially started my journey toward earning my health coach certification and I was going to pay for it using my DoorDash earnings. I figured, OK, $200 a month is only $50 a week. I can do that.

In the initial phone call with Katie, she told me how in six months, I could become a certified health and life coach. You can start getting clients as early as your second month in the program. My goal was to learn as much as I could, do all the steps and start going after clients by my second month into the training.

I started my classes in May. One of the most unique things was that I got to connect with different people all over the country. Once you started your assignments, you had to go to the Facebook group in your cohort and find a skills lab partner. My cohort was BHC (Become a Health Coach) May 2018. I got to meet up with people, talk to them over the phone, do assignments with them and report back how our sessions went.

The Health Coach Institute had great personal development practices for students taking the course. I really didn't expect all of that, nor did I expect how deep I would search within myself during the process. My first few skills labs were cool. I learned quickly that most of the people in HCI were white women, and this was the first time I was really just introduced to such a different lifestyle.

While I was studying to become a health coach, I was still traveling and enjoying the summer. I think that was what was also very appealing to me—I didn't have to be stuck in one place learning. Tiarra and I went to Virginia Beach and Atlanta countless times. We traveled all over just to eat different vegan food and to get out of Charlotte. It was a great change of pace because for so many years prior all my traveling was for work.

Being in the health coaching program or what we called BHC, I began noticing the benefits of investing in myself. One day, the thought came to me that if I wanted to make more money as an entrepreneur, and also buy more bitcoin, I need to reinvest some of this bitcoin into myself. I was falling in love with investing in myself. Though I had already been developing myself throughout this entire journey, I wasn't focused on how and what to specifically invest in until now.

While studying to become a health coach, I got word from Zay about a Black Bitcoin Conference being held in Washington DC. The event was organized by the Bitcoin legend Sinclair Skinner, who co-founded a company called I Love Black People. One of his main initiatives is bringing information about bitcoin to the African diaspora. I knew Mr. Skinner from a show I did with Miller-El and Bitcoin Murex Solutions. I reached out to him to learn more about the conference and I asked if I could come to speak. I didn't think he would actually say yes—but he did.

By September 2018, I was preparing to head to Howard University in Washington DC to speak on a panel at the first-ever Black Blockchain Summit. As I boarded the plane, I called my cousin Trey and told him what was happening.

"Bruh, this is crazy," I said. "I've been home four years, two of those four years I really just started getting into Bitcoin, and now I'm about to speak at a conference."

"Man, things take off fast," Trey said. "Just keep going and don't take your foot off the gas."

Around this same time, the coaches at HCI send out a message about doing a spring cleanse. I'm thinking, alright, what's this spring cleanse? The spring cleanse was something HCI did throughout the entire program for all students. They teach you how to facilitate the cleanse so you can coach other people to do it. The goal of the cleanse was to reset the body.

This was like on-the-job training, because we were then able to sell this to clients while we coached them. I was really excited about getting started. I remember making my first post about it on Facebook and instantly one of my homeboys purchased it, and then another one.

I was selling my cleanse for $197. Some of the other students thought that was a bit much, however I didn't think so. I was into selling my stuff higher than most other people because I was attached to it, and I knew I would deliver a high-quality experience. I had that Mayweather mentality about myself. The best way to describe it is this: From the beginning, you let people know you are valuable and that you have quality that comes with the work you do.

In Washington DC, I have a lot going on. I'm at the conference meeting people; I have a client for my health cleanse client, and I have a practice client as well. My first practice clients were my mom and my friend Anita. Practicing with my mom and friend allowed me to realize I didn't need to be coaching family members.

While I was at Howard University, I would sneak off to quiet areas to meet with my cleanse clients, then head to a panel speaking about how Bitcoin was changing my life. I also spoke about some projects I was working on with Murex.

One project was creating a Lightning Node. This was a project we had started on at the beginning of 2018 as a way to hold up the Bitcoin network. The network was running entirely too slow after a massive bull run. This was some high-tech stuff. I never thought about it at the time, but I was working on cutting-edge technology with no coding background. The thought alone was pretty dope. Bitcoin itself was still brand new, and now we had to have an upgrade. Coding was something rigorous. I had a newfound respect for coders. It takes a different level of patience to do coding, and it stretched my brain like never before.

At the conference, a few people had heard of lightning, but it was so new most even those who'd heard of it never thought about putting a node together. It was very unique to see what other people were working on, and what their passion was in this space. Overall, the experience in Washington DC was very cool. I made some great connections, met some dope people and had a great time.

After the conference, I was home for two days before traveling again. This time, Tiarra and I headed to San Antonio for her birthday to meet her dad. We even rented a white mustang from the website Turo, and drove to Houston. I met her dad, his wife and their family. It was really hot, we ate vegan food the entire time and stayed in various Airbnbs. I started noticing the joy people can get from traveling. Within a short period of time, I traveled so much that I woke up in Houston thinking I was in DC.

After leaving Texas, I went back home and focused on finishing my certification. My goal was to get my certification in six months. That would be the highlight of 2018. I put hours upon hours of work into this certification, and the day I got my certification, I felt like I finally had accomplished something. I compared it to getting my degree, because I never finished college.

When I completed the certification, it was just in time. The institute hosted an event called HCI Live. It was similar to a business conference, however it was for the participants in the program in Austin, Texas. While in Austin, I met a lot of people, but it was a little strange and outside of my element. I was at this hotel conference made up of like eighty percent white women. Even though it was something unfamiliar, I knew it would be beneficial. I didn't care how uncomfortable it was. I was there for growth.

HCI Live was absolutely a great experience. The very first day I got called on stage to get coached by one of the co-founders, Stacey Morgenstern. It was the first time I was in a room full of people who were a different race than me who I felt actually wanted to see me win. It was very strange. I almost didn't want to leave because I knew the outside world was nothing like this.

Despite those feelings, I decided to open myself up to new ways of living, different ways of building a career and new perspectives. I knew to be one of the best coaches in the world, I had to learn to become multicultural and step outside what I felt to be normal.

During the three-day event, I met with all my skills labs partners. I remember running into one of them at the airport. One of my favorite skills labs partners was a woman named Marjorie. She actually turned out to be one of the best people I met. She was really in tune with herself, nature and was a true free spirit. She saw the world from a different viewpoint, one of care, love and accountability. I knew she was making a great impact on her coaching clients.

That was one of the things that made you stand out in coaching: impact. Coaches consider the type of impact they leave on people. Do people feel more empowered? Or do they feel small and defeated? Those were a couple of things noticed that separated certified coaches, and people who were just coaching. HCI was a part of the International Coaching Federation, so their program—and the coaches it produced—had to be up to par.

On the last day of HCI Live, a woman named Chris came to greet me, shake my hand and say that it was a pleasure to meet me. The last day of the program they pick a winner of the $10,000 sales challenge. After they announced who the finalists were, Chris went on stage. Come to find out she was last year's winner. She then tells her story about how she went from a hundred dollars to $150,000 in a year. I was like, *damn*, who is this woman?

Afterward, she announces the current winner, we celebrate and proceed to do some practice coaching sessions. I asked her to do a session with me, and at the end of our session, she told me something that was very key.

"How do you envision your business?" she asked.

"I don't think a lot of people buy from me," I said. "I know it's going to be hard."

She immediately stopped me and said, "That's a limiting belief! When you have limiting beliefs, it affects all points of business. It affects your health and affects everything you do. If you want to be great at this, you have to search, find and remove all your limiting beliefs you have about yourself, because those are what really hold you back."

I was shocked. She was *really* good at this, and I wanted to be that good.

While at HCI, they were pushing a Mastery Program, which was the next level of coach training. It was on my mind the entire time I was there. Everybody had these great stories about Mastery. Once again, I met with another how-am-I-going-to-do-this situation. Then I just said, "Fuck it. Do it." I told the HCI folks, if they called me when I got home and came up with a plan, I would take full advantage.

* * *

When I got home from HCI Live, I googled places I thought would be friendly toward a health coach who wanted to give a talk. HCI had given us these templates to help us give business talks. I found this place called Lake Norman Salt Spa. The receptionist was very cool and allowed me to set up a time for December.

Ever since I was a child, I loved talking on stage. It was said that doing talks would be the fastest way to grow your business. December was too far to wait though. I remember trying to set up a talk at Whole Foods, and it got postponed. Another place called Central Food Hub, where vegan vendors sold their products, let me do a talk about kicking sugar. I nervously read from a sheet of paper the entire time, but I knew the only way to get over the nerves was to do the damn talk.

I didn't know I would be so well received, but it actually went really well. It gave me the confidence to go talk at Lake Norman Salt Spa. There was a smaller crowd at the spa, however that was better, because I was able to connect with people even more. The connection paid off because it was at Lake Norman Salt Spa where I signed up my first client for a total of $1,800—$599 a month for three months. And that was the start of me being a professional health coach.

Mastery

Early on, I realized doing talks was one of the best ways to get clients. I noticed that every time I did a talk, I got some type of client, momentum or made connections. I knew I needed to repeat this process as much as I could, however I needed to get better at what I was doing. Doing a talk was very powerful. I just didn't realize how powerful it was. I was out there just rambling, but I realized I needed to purposely gain more clients with these talks. People talk on stages all around the world, however you have to actually say something worth listening to and compelling enough for people to buy into you, to like and trust you.

HCI was key for me in growing my business and myself. Once I officially signed up for the Mastery Program I was eligible for the Mastery Retreat in San Diego, California. It would be my first time ever going to California, and that was just part of my excitement. The other part was the opportunity to network and be around people in the same profession as me. I knew I was about to be around some high-level individuals.

The first day of the retreat I started seeing just how next-level things were. The first part of my coaching certification, the focus was on enhancing behaviors and habits and recognizing self-sabotaging behaviors in ourselves. We were taught how to hold the space for our clients and help them see how they have been responsible for everything that has ever taken place in their lives. Later, it started getting more personal, like how you view yourself and what you believe about yourself, including deep set beliefs that could come from childhood traumas we all have.

The first day, we got right to work with two coaches Carey and Stacy, who ran the event. We instantly started talking about how by updating your beliefs, you can change yourself. One of the greatest paradigms I ever heard in my life was:

"Your beliefs create your experiences and your experiences confirm your beliefs."

HCI was always teaching paradigm shifts. The paradigms were to give you a different way of viewing what you were experiencing in the world, in your life and how you are completely 100 percent responsible for what has taken place. I was just taken aback. We kept the same atmosphere we had at HCI Live with open-style coaching sessions. At one point, a woman was called on stage. I remember this woman because my card had just been declined and she gave me ten dollars to pay for my meal. I was very happy because I was still trying to figure out how to make money in my own business.

I watched her being coached on stage, divulging her childhood. Stacy would always say, all of life's data is stored in what we like to call the "critter brain" or what some call the subconscious. It's always there in your life, always making decisions based upon what is taking place in the subconscious. Hearing that just freaked me the hell out. The woman started sharing some memories of her dad and how she took what her dad told her and it shaped her life. This particular tucked away memory was guiding her decision making subconsciously. In this exercise, she learned she held onto her dad's words and created a negative meaning from them. She tried her best to make a positive out of the negative, but the negativity was too much to overcome.

One thing we learned in Mastery was that as a child you accept every parental action to mean love. So if you slap your child, your child is going to perceive that as love. Even some of the most heinous actions, like sexual molestation, a child might perceive as love in the first few years of life. So you really have to be careful what you say to your child. I had a moment myself where I stood up and said, "What you shared now is making me think how I need to speak to my daughter." Marleigh was about to turn three that year.

I started noticing just how deep childhood trauma can affect people even into adulthood. The words parents speak to a child can affect how they turn out. Those words become their reality. Whether it's positive or negative, they are going to take that learned behavior in their adulthood. I'll pose a question for you: What things did your parents tell you as a child that you held onto? What do you hold onto even now, that you know is not the best for you, but you hold on to it still?

We did a lot of studying around our decision-making process. Many of the decisions we make are based upon not wanting to hurt our family members or hurt the people who raised us. With this approach, however, we can hurt ourselves because we go against what we truly want. When I realized that, I had a true revelation. You can live the life you want and still love your parents, but let go of the negative things you once held on to without feeling guilty for it. The reason you hold onto negative beliefs from parents is because you feel guilty. They raised you and you might feel like you owe them.

All of that was covered just on day one. We also learned how to have a "close the deal" conversation. They give you a script to follow and you had to learn the script well enough to use it and book a client. The closing the deal piece was one of the hardest things for me to understand. I realized learning to close the deal was a part of entrepreneurship and part of being a coach. My deal-closing skills, however, were terrible. In spite of this, was very adamant about one thing: I knew if I failed a lot and failed often, I would start picking up the pieces I needed to succeed.

This was very hard for me. During the retreat I had like four or five closing the deal calls set up. Every call people told me they were not interested in my coaching. I started really thinking, what the hell am I doing wrong? After getting rejected so many times, I got upset because shit was not coming across how I wanted. I knew I needed to really hone in on this or I was not going to really be able to make it. I was in the Survivor Trap. I wasn't really being the true essence of me. I was too busy caught up in thinking, damn, I need the money. Damn, I need the money. Damn, I need the money. Plus I was just a rookie. I thought it would be so much easier, but I learned closing the deal was more than just people jumping at the chance to work with me. Negotiations are critical, and I had to learn just how critical they are.

Bitcoin Lightning Node

This entire section is an Orca Moment that took place in 2018. One of the most tremendous events that year happened with Bro Miller-El and Murex Bitcoin Solutions. We were focused on creating solutions for the Bitcoin blockchain and solutions for people of the African diaspora to flourish with this new technology.

Miller-El and the rest of the brothers in Murex wanted to stay on the cusp of cutting–edge information. One thing I noticed happening with us as black people was that we are always last to adopt the latest technology. We like doing what's always worked instead of taking chances on something new. A lot of people in those days didn't see Bitcoin as something important, and that was terrifying.

What I loved about this experience was we set out to try to create lightning nodes. We did so not only for the Bitcoin network but also to teach others how to create their own nodes. This was brand new to everyone, even the people with coding experience. The lightning network was just introduced to the Bitcoin network. Even bitcoin was only nine years old at the time.

Some of the guys had some type of coding experience, but not me. Outside of creating a MySpace account in the early 2000s, I had no coding experience. This was something very new to me, but something I looked forward to learning. One of the first things we created was a Bitcoin node. It was a tedious process that took a lot of patience. You know, to create any type of coding platform meant you had to know a coding language and I didn't know any of that stuff.

The first thing I did was buy a Raspberry Pi, a monitor, USB cords, and a scan disk. When I first got the Raspberry Pi, I was like, wow, this is really how people move through the entire internet. They just use this little motherboard chip. It was rather amazing. It exposed me to what technology was on a very barebones level. Everything else is just a friendly user interface, but this was the real backbone of technology.

When I received the materials, I was told I had to learn how to use the Linux computer operating system. This entire process was brand new to me. We went to a site called Github and followed a coder named Stadicus. This guy had given out the blueprint to create a Raspberry Pi lightning node. This process was tedious and methodical. One wrong move could create a problem for weeks. When it happened to me, I really saw what it was like to be on the cutting edge of Bitcoin technology. We were simultaneously creating and updating this technology. It was our way of contributing to the bitcoin community.

This is why I always say decentralization is the best thing about Bitcoin. No one is the overseer but you. It is your total responsibility to contribute to this network. I dealt with Bitcoin on a very fundamental level. That's what gave me the confidence and the insight to know everything it took to participate in Bitcoin—beyond what the media was speaking about.

I got as far as creating the bitcoin lightning node and a wallet all using the Raspberry Pi. I learned how to do a little bit of programming. I learned how to work the backend of a computer. I learned coding languages used in Linux, and it was very top-notch to me. I had no idea all this went into coding. We even got as far as creating a test net for a lightning node and payments. Then my mind started shifting. I noticed every time I put myself into a complex bitcoin situation, I felt like my IQ increased twenty points. That's because this is where I learned the true essence of bitcoin and its complexity.

This entire experience opened my mind to many things:

1) **Coding or creating a new technology doesn't happen as quickly**

as people think. Being on the cusp of something as cutting edge as Bitcoin and a lightning node, means you have to go through bugs.

3) **Programming is just like life itself;** You start with a foundation and you build on that every day as much as possible. There will be hiccups. Sometimes you can find those solutions very quickly and other times you have to dig a while. We had a saying every time we ran into trouble in coding: Google is your friend. It amazed me how Google really had the answer to almost anything.

At this juncture in my life, I knew I had to build some valuable skills. What's more valuable than increasing the knowledge of your own brain? I never got to run a full lightning node. What I did learn however was, what we call in Bitcoin, how to decentralize. I also gathered a great deal of patience, a trait that was going to help me along this journey dealing with Bitcoin, being an entrepreneur and also in life.

The reason I deemed this entire chapter an Orca Moment is because of the following:

1) **We worked together.** At the beginning of the book, I mentioned orcas work in pods.

2) **This endeavor was highly sophisticated and very technical.** We had to use parts of our brain that some had never used before.

3) **We learned a value-adjustment.** We learned new ways of relating to bitcoin. No longer was price an issue. What we cared about was making sure the network would always stay decentralized.

I noticed getting top-quality knowledge does take time, however, it does pay off tremendously for years to come. Building a Bitcoin node (and attempting to build a lightning node) was one of the greatest learning curves I'd ever experienced, but one that I would never trade for anything in the world. It also trained me to always strive to build something lasting, and to be an early adopter. Once you're an early adopter, you gain a great foundation in the industry or technology. And when the consumers do come in, you'll be well prepared for them.

Doing this set me up for the future on a different level. I had no technical experience. This was something I didn't study in college. All we had was hardcore learning and application. That right there is what it takes to succeed in anything in life. No matter where you are in life, dedication to a process is always the secret to success.

Networking

During my first year coaching people said there were four ways to grow your business: talks, referrals, email and networking. To be honest, I used to have this great fear of networking. I never really knew what the hell networking was on a real level, but that was all the fuel I needed to start doing it.

Orca Moment: Always step towards fear. That's where the greatest rewards live.

I needed to see how I would do in a networking setting, however I didn't really know where to find networking events. I remembered I had the Eventbrite app on my phone. I usually used it for parties during CIAA, but I decided to give it a shot. I typed "networking" in the search bar. I found an event in downtown Charlotte that was happening in two days, and I quickly registered.

When the day came for me to go, I was nervous as hell. This particular event was held at a coworking space called Spaces. This was my introduction to the professional world. I walked into Spaces in downtown Charlotte. The place was filled with professional-looking people, men in business suits and women in the same type of attire. I walked in the door and didn't even know what I was supposed to do. I'd never been in this position before. I never had to network. I didn't even know what a network was. I stood at the door trying not to look nervous when this guy walked up to me.

"Hey man, how are you doing?" he asked.

"I'm alright. Just checking things out."

"Well, I'm John."

John tells me he is a life insurance agent who specialized in "defense financial planning."

Without even thinking I said, "I'm willing to learn about it."

I didn't care what he was selling. If he had knowledge and or services that I could use to better myself, I was all for it. Since the start of that year, I told myself I was committing to doing next-level stuff, especially when it came to improving my finances. Finances were important and having an education on how to properly plan was going to be very crucial for me to get to the next level in my life. Having bitcoin taught me that I needed my money to do something for me, but I knew there was more to having money than just that. I needed money for a legacy. That was the thing I kept thinking about.

Even dating Tiarra at that time was very tough, because we did not have the correct mindset about money. We were just going by what family and friends told us not knowing that everybody was playing the "broke game" or were "just over broke." Many were in this cycle of having a job, getting a check, paying some bills, having some fun, then being down on their luck again. I did not want to continue this same financial cycle.

After I talked with John awhile, he said he would take me around to meet some people. I thought to myself, what the hell am I going to do with people or say to them? John introduced me to a few people and I shook some hands. I didn't have any business cards on me, because at this day in age, business cards are a complete waste of time.

One of reasons I didn't go out to network was because I didn't think white people would do business with me—ever. I didn't understand how to do business on a more professional level, because when I was doing Vegan On The Go, reaching out to people was just tragic.

Eventually, I realized I had to just get out there and meet people. To make it easier on myself I focused on just collecting business cards. As I did this I noticed this networking event was just a bunch of entrepreneurial rookies like me and a few veterans who knew how to get clients. I realized that networking events were not really about networking, but were a way for you to try to get clients.

During this time, Eventbrite and MeetUp became my best friends. I was always there to see where the next networking event was. It started becoming part of my weekly routine. At one networking event, I met a young guy named Chris Wright. He had a company called Whistle, Charlotte's number one cleaning app company. Right out the gate we hit it off. He was young like I was and we were just trying to really figure out how to be entrepreneurs in our twenties. As I continued my networking journey, I saw him at another event in Charlotte at South Park Mall.

"Bruh, you're everywhere," I said.

"Yeah, I see you all-around man," he said. "You're out here really getting to it." We exchanged contacts and vowed to keep in touch.

At another networking event, I met a woman who said she was a branding specialist. I told her that I needed some branding, so we exchanged contact information. After a few days, we met at a restaurant and started sharing our stories. I told her about my business and my story. I never hesitated to tell people my situation.

"Well, I think I know someone who's better suited for you," she said.

She introduced me to someone who wanted to pass themselves off as a business coach. I won't mention his name, but he told me he could help with business development.

During our first conversation, he shared how he felt he could help get my business off the ground and grow. He also said he did some coaching himself. In my mind I was thinking working together might be a good idea, but I wasn't too sure yet if it would be. We scheduled another meeting, and things were going pretty cool. We had good conversations and even practiced some ways I could facilitate a sales process. I started noticing something that I learned from HCI. Since I was a certified health coach, I understood how deep coaching should be, and in our meetings he wasn't really coaching me on anything. I noticed early on that the value I was looking for wasn't there, however we signed a contract so I thought he may pick up eventually.

One thing I can admit is that he did help me create my LLC, but beyond that I didn't experience any high-level business coaching like I wanted. As a matter of fact, I remember at one point he told me I needed to read more. I told him I didn't mind reading since reading is what got me through prison and on this path of personal development in the beginning.

We met a few more times, and it was the same type of session. Since I was a coach, I could recognize that there was no real high-level coaching going on. At that time, I was very naive to business and how others conducted their business. I could feel there was a change coming.

One of those changes came when I started picking up books. One of the first books I started reading as an entrepreneur was a book called *Sell or Be Sold* by Grant Cardone. I saw his book on an Instagram ad, but before then I had never heard of him. The book title stuck out so much that I had to give it a shot. I only had to pay shipping and handling, so what else did I have to lose? Truth be told, I knew I needed some help, and if reading was going to be the thing that helped me, then I was ready to do that.

So as I'm reading this book, I'm getting all these great gems about the mindset it takes for someone to sell their product or services. I said to myself, damn, I'm getting some great info out of this book. I wonder what this coach of mine would have to say about this book? One of the greatest things I read in *Sell or Be Sold* was that you don't want to be deceiving. You don't want to lead people on the wrong path. You want people to know what they're doing with you, be up front and be a great individual. I took this to mean that you have to have some ethics. I'll never forget sitting in the office of this man who was supposed to be coaching me, sharing with him what I read out of the book, and he tells me to do the opposite. I didn't really like that, and the more we would meet, the more I noticed he didn't have time to meet with me. He would say some things like, "I got my other business going on. Let's meet up some other time. Let's set up another date." He'd make sure that bill will come, though, and I was just at a point where I knew this wouldn't last long at all. We weren't aligned on the same principles.

There comes a time when you notice a lot of people think they are something that they're not. I had good enough intuition to know that this man really wasn't who I thought he was. The more I learned, the more I started seeing the holes in his story. Luckily, when I did hire him, I closed my very first client. It was a referral from John, and the client paid me the first day we met. I was very happy and eager to get to work with her. Now I had a client, and this one client was just enough for me to be able to pay for my coaching program. I had a lot to learn.

I was very grateful for my client. She was a great person with a go-getter attitude. On my end, however, I didn't feel too confident after I bought this service from someone who didn't know what they were doing. That was something I could not deal with.

Branding

In the summer of 2019, I got a message from one of my coaching friends about a branding event. My friend wasn't able to make it, but she thought it would be something I should go to. I was open to doing damn near anything to raise my level of awareness. As soon as she sent me the web link to the event, I signed up. Immediately I received an email confirmation that said it was a free, all-day event and that I should bring my own food and come prepared to learn.

I'd never seen a conference or an event held this way, so I thought it would be very interesting. I forwarded my email to my friend Chris Wright who said he would go as well. It was cool because that meant I would know at least one person there.

I arrived at 8 a.m. to the hotel where the event was held. Once I walked in, I noticed the atmosphere. Not only did we have to wait in the lobby before sitting in the conference room, we had to sign in, and once inside, we couldn't use our cell phones. The main speaker was someone named JT Foxx. I'd never heard of him, however he was introduced as the number one business and wealth coach in the world. I said to myself, well, damn. How is he the number one business and wealth coach in the world and I've never heard of this guy? I'd heard of all the mainstream people, Grant Cardone, Brendon Burchard, Tony Robbins, however I'd never heard of this guy.

It was amazing to sit there and learn what business on his level. He was one of the more influential people who inspired me to strive to be the top one percent of the one percent. He talked about business in a very different way from other people. The first thing he talked about was how he traveled from country to country to speak. This made me feel like he had some credibility to talk about what he was about to share with us. He talked about how he speed reads through different articles and he always wanted to keep up with what was going on. He talked about mega branding from a top-down perspective, and he had all these crazy ideas that were so out of the norm.

This guy knew something about business most didn't. There's no way you have an eight-hour event for free and not know what you're talking about. He spoke about the power of having a coach, someone who you could invest in, who would in turn invest their time into you, so you can be the best version of yourself. He was very big on being about your business and being an international businessman. I remember him mentioning that you don't have to blow up in your hometown first to be successful. People who don't know you will always love what you're doing before people who know you will. I could see some truth in that. All the years I spent doing Vegan On The Go and educating on Bitcoin proved that to me. It was always people from different places who were quick to support me rather than people I already knew.

We sat in that room for eight hours, learned a lot and the entire time he was branding himself. He talked about how he always helped his clients level up. He was selling, without selling. He showed testimonials of his work and from his clients the entire time we were there. He also showed how people from all over the world would go crazy for the opportunity to work with him. I mean, people would just gravitate to him. When we got to the pricing part of his programs, they weren't cheap and he wasn't ashamed to tell you that he wasn't cheap. People still lined up to work with him.

JT Foxx showed me the difference between being a speaker and a closer. He said, "Most people would judge your speaking events by who's standing up and clapping for you when you're done. When I'm finished speaking, nobody can clap for me, because they're too busy buying my coaching."

I was like, damn.

During the entire event, he showed how much of an impact he made on people who had hired him as their business coach. JT Foxx knew the fundamental principles of human beings, how to build excitement, arousal and urgency to buy what he was presenting. He had a very different approach to business, especially branding. His focus was so heavy on branding because he believed that it makes the sales process easier. He would stress that if you can get on television to talk about your business, then get on TV as much as possible. It was all about branding and the perception you're building for yourself.

JT also stressed the fact that you should call yourself the best in your market. Brand and market yourself as number one, and have other people call you that, because it positions you as an authority, not just an expert. His stance on branding was so next-level. The better branded you are, the easier it is for people to want to do business with you, he said.

He was selling all kinds of coaching packages that cost as little as $5,000 and went as high as $20,000. I knew I wasn't there yet in my business—or life for that matter. I thought I was only going to walk away with the value he provided for free, until he offered a fifty dollar recording of his coaching and lessons to teach how to triple your income. It was a limited-time offer so I said, "Hell, let me get it now."

When he said it was a limited-time offer, that's exactly what he meant, because the minute we left, he took the offer down and the price went back to its original price. I see why he catches a lot of flak from people. Some think he's crazy. They think he does brainwashing on people to get them to buy his stuff. I don't know, and to be honest with you I didn't care. I was amazed because if you claim to be number one in the world and can back it up by showing the success your clients achieve just from working with you, it doesn't really matter how crazy your approach is. All that matters is the results you can provide the people who buy into what it is you are teaching.

I was grateful I sat there for eight hours because what he said transformed my business. JT put something different in the atmosphere. He showed you what it took to get to the top without all the hype and popularity.

I was very appreciative of this event because his way of working was just tremendous. It showed me that the world is much bigger than the country you're in. I recognized the power of being internationally branded. I walked away with the fire to strive to be one of the best of the best. His work and his words are even what led me to write this book.

After that event, I knew I was going to be able to reach a higher level. I was still working on ways to financially invest in myself. Since I didn't have money, I had to invest using my time. That was one thing I learned in prison. I had time. As long as I did something every single day to better myself, to better my business, the things I truly desired would start appearing.

Orca Moment: Even if you don't have money, you have time. Put in the time. Time is what's valuable. Time is the only thing that's valuable. You can get more bitcoin, you can get more money, but you can't get more time.

Memory

After leaving the event, I felt one thousand percent more confident to attend networking events. I figured, OK, I got a client from a networking event. Let's keep networking. I kept going out to different places, sometimes revisiting the same event over and over. It was cool to have the experience of networking, to get out there and get out of your comfort zone. If you have a fear of meeting people, or you have a fear of talking about your business, this is what you need to do.

Orca Moment: If you're afraid to talk about your business, how the hell are people ever going to know that you are in business?

Several days go by, and I get an Instagram message from my friend Vonte. This is the same Vonte who introduced me to Gucci Mane and also told me about Dyme Boxing. He always had an eye for great things. Vonte sent me an Instagram post of this place called The Charlotte City Club. Up until that point, I'd never heard of Charlotte City Club. I look it up and it seems to be very prestigious. As I had mentioned earlier, I had overcome this subconscious fear I had of trying to do business with white people. Living in Charlotte being an entrepreneur, you're surrounded by nothing but banks and finance companies. I wanted to be one of those coaches who did business with those types of businesses. I wanted to host workshops and corporate training for the employees, so I had to put myself in that type of environment.

After doing some research on the Charlotte City Club website, I found the person I needed to contact. I emailed her letting her know I was interested in coming to the Charlotte City Club and wanted to know what the procedure was for me to do so. She emailed me back immediately saying she was excited for my email and that they had a welcome night for all prospective members that week, and I was welcome to join. I emailed her back almost immediately to confirm that I would be attending.

The Charlotte City Club was downtown Charlotte at the very top floor of a building on West Trade Street. It's like nothing I've ever seen before. It looked a lot like Old Charlotte with a view that was absolutely amazing. The Charlotte City Club seemed to be made up of a lot of CEOs, high-level business people, and movers and shakers with a lot of connections. This was a different level of networking, and I didn't want to come across salesy. I genuinely went out there to just meet people and see what it was like. After being there for several hours, I made some connections, got some emails, and then the receptionist invited me to a wine tasting they were having the following week. She also said I could bring a friend.

I brought my business coach with me to the wine tasting event, however he ended up leaving shortly after arriving. I was by myself at this wine tasting, drinking all of this high-quality wine with nothing but middle-aged and older white people. I'm the only black man, and as I was tasting the wine I started thinking to myself, just how the hell did I go from being in prison to being here? It was a surreal moment.

While I was there, I connected with a young woman named Caitlin Grimes. I could tell she was younger than most of the people in the room, and she was very, very intelligent. She worked for a company that managed digital assets. All the younger people were sitting at the same table, in our own world, drinking this wine, and watching this man describe every bottle of wine he was selling. I know I drank more wine than I ever had in my entire life that day. Overall, it was a great experience, and networking over wine was definitely something I would repeat.

After the event was over, Caitlin invited me to another networking event called Velocity. Since going on my networking tour, I began to see different levels of entrepreneurship, but I wasn't getting a lot of clients. I was really winging it, and I was so caught up in networking that I figured I'd probably get a client somewhere by just doing this. That wasn't the case.

Ocra Moment: Take time to develop a strategy. Find someone who understands the business you're in and humble yourself. Learn what you don't know. You don't know what it takes to get to that next level, because if you did you'd be there already.

My first Velocity meeting went the same as the other networking meetings. We met up, people shared what their business does, who they are looking to work with and so forth. At this point, I still only have one client. All of this meeting and greeting was fun, however I was not making any money, and staying this course was rather rough. I started feeling like I was going in a big ass circle. I would send email, on top of email, on top of email getting to meet people. I would follow up doing all the stuff and then I started to ask myself, am I really doing all this for nothing?

I had a lot of things going on in my mind. How do I crack this nut? How is this happening? How are people making money with coaching? One reason I started venturing outside of my community was because it was hard for me to show black people the value of my skills. I was networking in different circles and the same thing was still happening. I was really getting frustrated with the whole ordeal. One positive thing out of going to the Velocity meetings was that the organizer, Will, helped us structure our "elevator pitch" for our business. He got you comfortable talking in front of people, and I was very grateful for that.

After a while I started thinking, I'm trying to get some clients. I have this great program. I even switched my niche from being a health coach to a mindset coach. At HCI, we had a $10K in ten weeks competition. We were given ten weeks to boost our sales and hone in our sales pitch. At the end of the competition, whoever had the best sales pitch and best sales presentation won $10,000. When the top performers were called on stage they would say, you really have to have a great niche and know your audience. When I first heard this I thought—like a naive entrepreneur rookie—that I knew my audience and I was ready to go.

Orca Moment: When you are learning something new or you're trying to achieve things you never have, don't underestimate it and think it's so easy to do. If it was easy, you would have already done it. So take the coaching with respect, and just know if you knew all of this already you would already have what you want.

By the summer of 2019, I was feeling really down. I was trying to land big deals with Fortune 500 companies and none of them had gone through. My mom's car got repossessed, Tiarra and I were not on the greatest terms, and I couldn't even pay my own "business coach," because I didn't have the funds. I wasn't making any money and was still DoorDashing even though I really wanted to quit.

Orca Moment: I was stuck in the mindset of thinking about what I did not have. I was stuck in the mindset of being a business owner— not an entrepreneur. I kept attracting what was on my mind the most: lack and scarcity. The more I thought about how negative it was, the more I attracted the negative.

After wallowing in my misfortunes for a while, I started to immerse myself in self-development and business strategy. I saw a lot of transformation happening with other HCI members, and I knew I could find something that could turn things around.

One day on Instagram, I saw a post asking if I would like to triple my reading speed, increase memory retention and turn on my super brain. I'm thinking, who the hell is this? It turned out to be a guy named Jim Kwik, a brain coach who was promoting his online brain training system. When I heard that I was hooked. I knew the value of learning online. I knew the value of coaching, but I also knew the power of the brain. I learned very well in prison that my ultimate power was I can learn anything. It's that mentality that kept me going as an entrepreneur because I knew I could do this. I was built for this. I watched my mom have her own business. I watched my uncle Herb have his own business, my Aunt Tanji was self-employed. Everyone in my family had an entrepreneurial spirit in them, and it was time for me to accept it was in me too. This is what I was meant to do, however it comes with a price that you will pay if you intend to succeed.

What really pushed me to buy Jim Kwik's masterclass was when he said, "Maybe you are in business and you need to memorize a sales process." I immediately thought, please just take my money *now*, because that's exactly where I was. Jim knew his audience. He continued to say, "Maybe you want to be more efficient, maybe you just want your brain to turn on to a different level. No matter what it is, this program is for you."

I looked at this program for a while before finally signing up. I knew I had a little bit of shiny object syndrome, but this was something different. The main reason I wanted to take this course was because I had a lot of books to read. I knew I needed to put in the time to make these books work for me, and I knew if I read these books, I could transform my business.

I remember JT Foxx opening his event by saying how much he read. He would speed read everything so he could have the competitive edge. Since I was a solopreneur, I felt I needed to open parts of my brain so I could perform at my best, at least until I could delegate responsibilities to others. I also felt this course would help me understand and operate Bitcoin better. Also, I wanted to teach my daughter, Marleigh, and my family what I learned.

I had a lot riding on this course and I attempted to get a huge return on my investment. I knew I could offer the knowledge I gained from this course to my clients as well. Not only could I provide them mindset coaching, but I could also help them increase their memory. One thing I learned from reading Grant Cardone books was that I was in the business of people, not products and services.

Orca Moment: Being an entrepreneur is more about knowing the workings of a human being, not just your industry.

The first day of Jim Kwik's course I immediately felt more intelligent than I ever had in my life. I felt like I could memorize anything I wanted. Jim made everything fun which made learning easy. Everything that was a challenge, I knew I could master—even something as complicated as Mandarin.

After several weeks of the program, I finally got to the section on speed reading and comprehension. Once I finally completed it, I felt like I could read anything and everything in sight. First, I read a lot of books on the power of the brain written by Daniel Amen. I also read the book *Moonwalking With Einstein* by Joshua Foer. While reading this book, I practiced new ways to take notes. I developed a very sharp eye for details and kept noticing the name Tony Buzan referenced. Tony Buzan was considered the godfather of memory.

I always wanted to know how some people achieved such great things and from my readings, I learned that they learn differently. They're always reading, reading and reading. I started just flying through books. I got to the point where I was reading ten books a month and applying what I read.

I started reading Tony Buzan who wrote about the power of mind maps. Once I learned the power of mind mapping, I had the ability to learn and memorize anything I wanted. With Jim Kwik's course and Tony Buzan's teaching on mind maps, I knew I had a superpower. I now had something to bring to the world.

Not long after this, I set up a memory enhancement workshop. The moment I did that, a lot of things started changing for my business. I was already a coach who was open to trying new things and challenging the norm, but now I had something golden. I could improve the sharpness of your mind, and I knew people would buy it.

Now, my marketing was still the same. I was using social media, but just re-worked what I did. The first workshop ever offered, I charged twenty-five dollars. What shocked me the most was a lot of people who paid didn't even show up. These workshops would last for about an hour, and I put together material that I knew would get people thinking about whether they were using their time and brain effectively.

I wanted to grow my workshops into something deeper, combining my mindset coaching skills with my newfound memory skills. I went all over Charlotte spreading the word, but things continuously fell on deaf ears. Still, I was getting more sales than I was previously.

During my journey of increasing my own brainpower I started really noticing the power of reading, applying what you learn and solving your problems faster. Because I could read so much and so quickly, I decided I wanted to read every book that Grant Cardone put out. I felt a new level of inspiration just reading his books and hearing him talk. His thought pattern on business was all about never giving up. It was all about quality and the quantity of effort that you put into what it is you want in life.

Power Circle

Once I completed the memory course, I started reading a book for every problem I needed to solve in my business. I exponentially increased my productivity. It was like the ultimate light bulb went off in my head. Things were going in a great direction for me.

Shortly after completing the course, I remember going to a networking event and running into Chris again. He told me about an opportunity to work at a coworking space, called CoWork by Camden. He said it had just opened in South End and that I should go check it out since they were always looking for new people.

I went to an open house event at CoWork. Luckily, no one was there. The vibe of the space, however, put me in a mindset that I knew I could get a lot done here. Brittany, the administrative assistant there, made CoWork seem like a magical place during our tour. After she told me about the first month's discount, I was ready to book the space. Then the reservation system let me save another forty dollars on top of the discount and I was thrilled. Before I left, Brittany said she looked forward to watching me grow my business at CoWork.

Getting the space at CoWork was a big step for me. I felt a sense of freedom to both work and create. This spot was open twenty-four hours a day and seven days a week. The space gave me some type of balance in my life, because I felt I could finally focus on *one* thing at a time, then go to the next.

Orca Moment: I remember reading in the book Pareto Principles about the 80/20 rule, and how focusing on the most important 20 percent will affect the majority 80 percent. I applied this principle to my brain. I figured if I increased how my brain performed, then I would naturally perform better at whatever I set my intention on.

I also remember bringing this concept to my clients when we were doing deep work on their beliefs about themselves. We had to uncover which beliefs were holding them back and keeping us from reaching our goals. For instance, a big belief of mine was always playing the victim. I believed it was my responsibility to do everything and was responsible for everybody else's finances.

* * *

I fell in love with increasing human productivity, which was affected by one's views of self, thoughts about circumstances, how your brain worked, the meaning you make of situations and the quality of life you maintained. My goal was to really build a coaching practice that helped people excel into the next level of life, to their highest level of performance. That was my goal in every program I built, every person I talked to, and even my goal for writing this book.

I learned everything by experience. I wanted to always strive to be the best. I never shied away from investing in myself, because it's how you're going to grow. I had to develop a strong sense of whose words were worth paying attention to and whose words I accepted as truth. I viewed myself as a fearless leader. I would read books on leadership and what qualities made leaders effective. The theme was always centered around rapport, and communication, so I would pick up books on those subjects and read as many as possible. I read books on social media, I read books on time management, and, more importantly, how to build a base of potential clients. Building a client base was something I was never really taught in a way that worked for me. People always talk about it here and there, but I needed to know how to actually build something for myself.

I was still struggling getting my name out and getting people to work with me. Grant Cardone, in his book *Sell or Be Sold*, says to develop a power base, because someone is out there, who you've probably known your whole life, who can open doors for you. After reading that, I started searching my phone, and I came across an old friend of mine named Trey Ward. We played amateur basketball together, and we used to spend the night at one another's house or ride with each other to basketball tournaments. I looked Trey up and what stood out the most was that he was only on LinkedIn. I reached out to him and he was happy to hear from me. We then set up a time to meet at CoWork. I felt like I had upgraded from meeting in coffee shops just because CoWork supplied free internet.

Trey and I spent about an hour at CoWork catching up. I told him my story and he was really glad to see that I was able to continuously grow during my life. After that, I told him what I was looking to do as far as coaching and building my business. Trey was big on going through nonprofits to make important connections in Charlotte. One of his connections was a man named Jamal Tate, who was really big in Charlotte's charity scene. I didn't have any interest in being involved in Charlotte's charities, but Jamal had a different approach to business, just like Trey.

Jamal was a very intelligent guy. We had a similar background with both of us getting into some trouble when we were young. The first time I reached out to him, he didn't email me back. I told Trey that I thought this was going to be a lost cause, but Trey came back and told me the reason Jamal didn't answer was because I used Trey's nickname, and not his real name, William. Once that was cleared up, Jamal contacted me every so often. Once we finally had a good conversation, he could tell that my heart was in the correct place, and that we could make some real moves. I shared with him that I wanted to use my memory and mindset coaching to teach to some of the at-risk youth in Charlotte as well.

Jamal and I ended up going to several community events in Charlotte where he introduced me to a lot of big names in the city. Jamal was a great partner. Iron sharpens iron and our situation was no different. We both wanted to work together to further not only ourselves but more importantly our community as a whole. We were always looking to build something, and that's when I really started understanding the importance of working with someone who compliments you and your skills. I actually experienced what it meant to work with someone as a team, and not just be all in it for yourself.

The first thing Jamal did was invite me to do some workshops with him at his program for non-violent first-time offenders. The first time I felt like it was an opportunity to give back my time and help the youth. I started to notice, however, that a lot of things weren't as forward-thinking as you might think.

I noticed these nonprofits had lots of programs designed to help people who looked like me, but their leadership didn't really want to let me—a black man—into work. It was a real gatekeeper mentality that I despised. In my mind, that kind of behavior showed you weren't fit to lead.

Orca Moment: You have to be fit to lead. You have to have the guts to take on what is uncomfortable. If you're not open to doing that, then you don't want to grow and you're not going to ever grow. You can not cake walk yourself into success. You can not cake walk your way into changing the lives of other people, because they can only go as deep as you're willing to go with yourself. If you don't go deep, and if you don't step out on that fear, you will keep your followers in the same mediocre box you are living in.

We started seeing this a lot in Charlotte at certain nonprofits, and it sickened me. It seemed like people just talked about change, and if the change didn't fit the norm, then it was ignored. Jamal helped open my eyes to what was really taking place in the city. I noticed a lot of people would talk about upward mobility, but not implement any type of program or structure to create change. I had a goal to teach my memory training and coaching to the groups that needed it most, but it was really rejected at all levels. I came to realize—thanks to my HCI training—that these non-profit leaders couldn't get past their own beliefs about black people. They were keeping themselves in the same mediocre box they believed they should continually be in. People would say, "We've done everything we can to help" when they really just did a lot to help. They never actually did *everything*, because if they had done *everything* they would have had a different result. People here didn't want results. They just wanted to feel good, to portray themselves as doing something to help. I came to this conclusion of a Harvard study that ranked Charlotte's upward mobility dead last out of fifty cities.

After being in the nonprofit scene, I finally saw why those numbers were real. No one was teaching anything that would increase productivity in people. Everyone wanted to take a safe, mediocre approach. No one wanted to take that next step.

Excuses

J amal introduced me to the Champions Networking group, which was full of corporate executives or people who sat on boards of big nonprofits. I really didn't know what to expect. The first meeting was at a J.P. Morgan Bank in Charlotte. Charlotte was one of the top three banking cities in the country. Every bank you could name was stationed in Charlotte and everyone was moving here to do some type of work with banking or finances.

Even though I still was not heavy in the nonprofit space, I at least wanted to give it a shot and step up and meet new people. I did my best not to really interact with this scene for quite some time. Before meeting Jamal, everyone just kept warning me about nonprofits. Some would say, "There's an opportunity to do good work, but they don't ever want to pay you what you're worth, let alone the value of the service you provide."

As great as these people were as individuals, as a group, it was a bit different. I started noticing that matter what position someone might have in their industry, you will always have people who are doers and people who are talkers. This reminded me of something Kobe Bryant once said in an interview on YouTube. He said in the NBA "you have guys who are just there because they're good at basketball. You have guys who are there just to get a check or change the situation of the family, but you only have a small few who want to be great."After hearing this I applied that framework to everything around me. There was a small group of business guys who I felt really wanted to do something, to go that extra mile to make change.

Going to all these events and experiencing some of the roadblocks I did, it started making sense why some would say it takes years to start really making money in your business. I realized the benefit of having a coach. Going out into business blind without guidance will have you running around in so many circles. I guess this is why people say you have to be brave to be an entrepreneur. You are really working day after day to obtain the fruit of your labor that you won't see for a few years into the future.

I started noticing the differences between those who were striving to be great, and those who were just there for a payday. The conversations were different, the energy was off. For those who were just looking to get paid, it seemed like every obstacle was a sign to look elsewhere because it didn't go correctly the first one thousand times. It was very sad to be honest. I had no clue how some people were being called successful with that type of mentality. I was noticing how far I had come mentally, and how much further I had to go. This, I feel, is the difference between being a shark, and an orca: paying attention to the tiny details.

Everywhere I went, I wanted people to know that I was here to change the world, even if I didn't know how I was going to do it at the moment. I knew I had the missing factor that would create change for the community of people who deserved it the most. I didn't feel enough was going to ever be done by the people who were currently in power. Most of those people were too far removed from the equation, even if they had a tough childhood. They were kind of like the CEO who was out of touch with his workers. After making $500,000 a year and being twenty years removed from his rough upbringing, he'd still be out of touch with the problems of today.

I also felt some of the leaders had too much sympathy instead of the correct amount of empathy, which breeds too much acceptance of excuses. At first I was sickened by it. Excuses and I have never been friends, even when I subconsciously catch myself making them, it irks me. I then have to step outside myself and get it together. I despised excuses so much that sometimes I wouldn't even sit down to return a phone call or email someone if I heard them making too many excuses. I viewed excuses as a hole that needed to be filled with knowledge on a particular topic, so it could no longer be an excuse. I know some people say I'm a bit crazy, but people with crazy success don't fall victim to excuses.

Orca Moment: Notice when you're in a conversation and you hear someone give excuses and you agree with it for the sake of conversation. Don't worry, we all have done it. The only way to limit those types of conversations is by surrounding yourself with people who don't make any excuses.

Coaching

I was reading through books like crazy. I read about how to build a business, communication, sales and leadership. I read more than twenty books in about five months. I started learning what a business was and what your main goal should be. Your focus as an entrepreneur is to solve problems. The world has a lot of problems to solve and you need to find out which ones you can solve. When I came home from prison, I would work all these crazy manual labor jobs, but people would always want me to solve complex problems. From that, I learned that a gift of mine was problem-solving. I've always enjoyed problem-solving as a child, but prison amplified it. Even though we were in somewhat of a box, or a cage, I didn't allow my mind to get locked up. It's like Young Jeezy said in a song, "lock my body, but can't trap my mind."

I wanted to build my coaching practice on solving complex problems in my clients' lives and beyond. I looked up to some of the great entrepreneurs of our time like Jeff Bezos, Peter Thiel, Elon Musk, Steve Jobs and even athletes who turned into entrepreneurs like Kobe Bryant and Floyd Mayweather. On one end of the spectrum they were great at what they did, but why were they great? How were they stepping up to the plate better than everyone else? I wanted to answer those questions. I fell in love with the process of amplifying the human experience, and that's what I wanted to do for people in my business.

I always had guides along the way whether it was prison, life, or business.

Bettering oneself is all about noticing what you are missing or what you are not doing, or even what you don't know how to do. For this to happen, an extra person is needed for guidance. If you try to operate with the mentality of, "I can do it all on my own" then you will fail miserably.

That was my first order of business—get coaching. Secondly, I realized I knew something about business, but I had a lot of major gaps to fill. I had this vision of what success looked like, what winning looked like. I knew I had a vision but was missing a solid plan to get there. I didn't want to continue operating off of raw talent. I remember reading the book *Atomic Habits* by James Clear. In it, he stressed the point that you have to create a system. He made a great comparison to sports, saying that teams don't focus on the scoreboard. They focus on the system. Systems are what built winners.

Finding my own system was what I was looking to accomplish by reading so much. I was taking bits and pieces of knowledge from every single book I read, and creating the business. I read books on things I knew I sucked at such as closing deals, negotiations, sales process, building rapport and mindset shifts. I started noticing what it took to really be this orca. You have to work on those underlying things that are not talked about. Those misconceptions and beliefs you have about yourself. You have to become aware of what's going on in your brain's subconscious.

When I was reading the book *Incognito* by David Eagleman he stressed the fact that the brain runs more on the subconscious than anything else in the world. There's an argument to be made that every decision isn't really your conscious decision. Instead, it's one that was put together in the subconscious of your mind.

By reading these high-level books, I was living out what I told myself when I was in prison. I vowed that if I would ever go back to school or take a course on something I wanted it to be extremely difficult and of high quality. After that, I would go out and dominate that area and be the best at it.

At HCI, I learned how to stay healthy. We really dialed in on what was going on in the background of the mind. This allowed me to realize I was responsible for everything that took place in my life. For instance, there were times me and my mom would argue about finances. I shared this with an HCI success coach named Kim who told me the honest truth.

"Justin, you are operating off of hurt from your childhood," she said. "That's why you still have these arguments. Yes, it sucks, however you can tell the younger version of you that we no longer need to hold on to that pain, and that it's time to ultimately take control over it."

That was some of the greatest coaching I ever received. Once I applied her advice, I knew results would not be automatic, but over time I would see the value in what we discussed. These were the types of conversations I knew successful people were having. Ones that centered around responsibility over everything, because increasing your responsibility is how you grow. This is what I knew was missing from other programs or leaders who wanted to create change in people but they didn't know how.

In order to make change happen with your current situation, you have to be willing to be different, feel different, expose yourself to the unknown parts of your mind and remove those chains of bondage that hold you back. People are very passionate about thinking you have to hold on to who you once were. This is very much a misconception. I know this because my coach, Jen and those in our mastermind group, were constantly reprogramming old beliefs. Some of us in our twenties—probably younger than that—never "grew up" the toddler within ourselves. When I learned about the inner toddler, I knew that this type of knowledge could grow not only my community, but the world, and anyone who was really ready for change.

Growth

I met Jen Gaudet at the HCI Mastery Retreat in 2019. After I shared my life story, Jen approached me saying she had the perfect idea for me. She told me I should work with young black youth and share my story and struggles with them to inspire hope and change. I could tell Jen was really serious about this and that she was serious about me growing as an entrepreneur.

I knew Jen was on the same wavelength as me when she saw a picture I posted with JT Foxx. After one of his mega branding events, we posed together for a picture which I quickly posted on Facebook. Not even a minute after the post, Jen likes the post and leaves a comment saying, "Isn't he amazing!!!" I immediately messaged her and said, "Yes! And how did you enjoy the event?" Long story short, she told me she hired him. I thought, whoa, what the hell? I had this reaction for several reasons, however the main reason was after I left his mega branding event, I knew I didn't have the funds to hire him. I wasn't worried though because I knew that one day I would work with him. I still believe I will make it happen.

Orca Moment: Never doubt yourself, it's hard to do in the beginning, however I as long as you tell yourself you can do, and believe and act on it the "how" will slowly reveal itself.

Jen saying she worked with JT was direct confirmation that I was in the correct alignment, however, I needed to up my game and improve. After that conversation Jen, we stayed in touch either by phone or by social media.

It took me several months to actually meet with a group of young black men. When I finally did, it was at a nonprofit called The Males Place in Charlotte. I was offered to come speak to them about what I was doing with my memory work, so I did a workshop. Afterward, we took a picture. It really was a joyful event to watch young black children notice the power of their brains, and how there are more ways to learn than what they are taught in school.

Once I posted the picture, Jen immediately messaged me and made a connection for me to be on a podcast with a woman named April. I felt that was her way of applauding me for acting on her suggestion. I could tell I could confide in Jen and she was ready to serve.

Jen delivered tough love better than anyone. I remember when I finally was so tired of trying to do things by myself that I reached out to her to inquire about coaching. Her words let me know I was headed in the correct direction. She said, "Are you ready to get out of your own way, Justin?"

My first reaction was how am I in my own way? I'm doing everything right. However, that was from my own point of view, not from an expert who was on the outside looking in. Jen shared that she was starting a six-month mastermind program for coaches. I told her I'd do it. I told Jen I felt like I was Kobe and she was Phil. I knew the power of working with her was going to be life-changing and I was ready for the ride.

I immediately saw the value in working with Jen. I noticed the power of the law of attraction. I would tell Jen how much of a reader I was, how I read all types of books, but kept falling short with money and didn't know why. As you can see I was always on a journey of improvement when it came to finances. She told me since I loved reading so much, I should check out a book called *Profit First*. Once I purchased the book and read it, I instantly realized the power of the person of who I was working with. Our work was definitely about to be transformational.

I soon learned that in order to make more money, you had to do a lot of personal development. The power of reading started becoming very important because what I read would play out in my day-to-day life. I realized how the power of the mind really worked: what you put in is what you get out.

Orca Moment: *Your mind is a projector of what you put into your brain. Think of your brain as a movie theater. When you look up toward the back ceiling, you see the projector. Now, what's going on behind there is the subconscious. What's loaded into that projector are the images you see, and the images you see is your consciousness. This is what reading and listening to successful business people taught me.*

I purposely put myself in different networking circles with high-performing people so my subconscious could take it all in and make the thoughts I needed to succeed. This is something I learned from reading *Incognito* by David Eaglemen. I remember when I was at JT Foxx's mega branding event and he said you want to get on TV as much as possible to brand yourself. I didn't know how this would happen, but I knew it could.

I met a brother named Kevin who had a publicity company called SideReelBranding. He managed clients and helped them get their story out to the world. Kevin was a journalist who used to work in TV production and had a big network of journalists—black journalists at that—who he worked with. One day he invited me to a holiday soiree for me to meet some of his contacts including other journalists. Once I arrived, I saw a lot of TV anchors who I grew up watching as a child. I was kind of star-struck to be honest. I felt like I was moving up the hidden ranks of networking.

Once everyone was seated and acquainted, Kevin introduced me to everyone. People then started to mingle when a woman introduced me to an interesting connection.

"This is Amanda and she is amazing," the woman said. "She's gotten me on TV in Charlotte, Greensboro, DC, and Atlanta."

I made a mental note of what the person said about her and I knew I had to connect with her. This is around the end of 2019, and as we were approaching a new decade, my mine concern was how I would get myself out there. What am I going to do differently that I didn't do before? I knew I needed to find someone who could help me push this message out to people because I was struggling doing it on my own.

At the end of the soiree, I got Amanda's information. She was rushing out the door, but I managed to grab her number. I was at a point now in my business where I was making a steady $1,200-$1,600 a month. It wasn't much, but it was a ten-fold increase from $150 a month—my previous income. After being in Bitcoin for three, going on four years now, I knew the percentage of monetary appreciation is what mattered the most.

I knew if I could grow from $150 to $1,500 in two years with little to no coaching, no real focus or strategy, then I knew with the correct things in place, along with my own knowledge and efforts, more exponential income growth was around the corner. I was saving my money in Bitcoin, and I knew I had to start getting in front of people on a different level. That process had to start with putting myself around people who I knew could help me get the results I wanted.

Even though I ran into a lot of dead ends from networking, I still had some pretty powerful people in my network. I started using my network to my advantage. I had to ask myself early on, what do you have going for yourself? I didn't have a crazy following on social media, I didn't even know what the hell email marketing was, but I realized everybody has something working for them in their favor. You just have to know what's working in your favor. You might see something that worked for someone else, and you may want to do that same approach, but you'll risk missing what comes to you naturally. And in the beginning of building a business *that shit matters*.

Jen told me this every time I was in the hot seat during our coaching meetings, she would end with, "Justin, lean into your network. That's why you have been networking this entire time. *Use the network.*"

I didn't have crazy social media followers or do email marketing, but I had a crazy powerful network. I had to start using that network to open up doors for me. This wasn't even about sales right now. It was mainly about introductions and getting my name and story out there.

Once I started using my network to open doors for me, a lot of other things started opening up for me. Early on I didn't notice how powerful networking was, because I was so one-track-minded about networking. I had a shark mentality. However when I started shifting my mind, and Jen started showing me the steps we often overlook to build our business, I knew networking was one of the most powerful things that helped me excel not just in business, but in life in general.

Networking is what I've done my entire life; I just never knew it. I made it harder than what it actually was, but you always do that when you operate from a place of not knowing. That's why it's important to always be in the know and improve your weaknesses.

Orca Moment: We don't live in a world where the answer "I don't know" or "I didn't know" will be repeatedly accepted. The internet has taken that to another level. Always seek knowledge.

I finally met up with Amanda and told her my story. I told her what I was passionate about, I told her what I was doing and she said she could possibly open a door for me to get on TV. I knew just being on TV didn't automatically mean instant money, however it was the start of the process. As Jen would say, "TV gets you a lot of fans. It's on you to turn them into buyers."

I desperately needed to get exposure and put myself in a position of power and authority. My goal was to be an authority, not the expert. That was always the goal. You want to be the one who the people in charge come to for knowledge. Like they say in old mafia movies, you want to be the boss of all bosses, the king of all beasts. In a room full of alphas you want to be the apex. In an ocean filled with sharks, you want to be the killer whale.

In order to do this, you have to discover where you are lacking, understand your weaknesses and look deep within yourself to try to create a solution.

If you don't go deep enough, you'll never find the true answers to your problems. You'll also notice when others aren't doing the hard inner work on themselves. You've got to go deep to get to the top. If you're reading this book, and you're an aspiring coach or leader, you cannot want something out of your clients, staff, or subordinates that you're not willing to put in the work for you to do for yourself.

2020

2020 started off very strong. By the very end of 2019, I was really going hard and crazy with reading. I ended the year by reading seven books in the month of December. I wanted to continuously push myself and my brain to the limit. I wanted to learn as much as I could about my brain, and be more efficient than ever. I didn't know it then, but I was damn sure going to need it heading into 2020.

While I was doing this self-studying, I continued looking at how I could bring this knowledge to the world. I met up with Amanda all the time. I told her I got invited to do a workshop at Friendship Missionary Baptist Church, the same place I did a talk the year prior when I was focusing on just health coaching. I was invited back this year to talk about something different. That year I decided to speak about memory and how memory could help people improve their quality of life.

That talk at Friendship Missionary Baptist Church was a surreal experience since that was the church my mother and I would go to when I was a child. Every time I talked there, I would see people who I remembered seeing growing up. The group I spoke to was the Women's Perspective Group of the church. After the talk was over, so many people came up to me and told me how much they enjoyed learning how powerful the mind can actually be when shown different learning techniques. The talk went so well I met a potential client. One woman approached me and said, "Hey, I think I need what you offer and I would love to work with you."

I even had Amanda meet me there to watch my talk. After the talk was over, she was very impressed. She said, "This is something we could work with. I could pitch this to different news stations to see if we can get you some exposure on the news and see how things go from there. Let's see how we can get you some business."

Amanda was a very nice person who definitely had deep connections. Not even a week after the service I was booked for a TV interview in Greenville, South Carolina. I got interviewed and taught some memory tricks to the anchors. When I arrived, I wasn't nervous at all. As a matter of fact, I knew I belonged here. This was my introduction to TV life, and I loved it. I really felt like I had arrived.

After I left the station, I remembered I had to get in contact with the woman who wanted to work with me at Friendship. She had a busy schedule but had agreed to meet with me at CoWork the same day as the news interview. Through our conversations, I found out that she had a very nice position at one of the biggest banks in the world. She explained that my story and presentation provided her value she hadn't seen before, and she was willing to give my program a shot. Ironically enough, I created this program the week before my talk at the church.

Orca Moment: I value preparation. You never know when a moment will come along. I learned early on as an entrepreneur to always be ready for any moment, because you don't want the moment to appear and you're fumbling around with an idea that's not ready. Always create and always be prepared...your day is coming.

When she told me she was willing to give my program a shot, I have to be honest, I was a bit nervous. Not because I didn't think it would be good for her, but because I never offered anyone a program for this amount of money before. I showed her the investment and she said, "OK, that's good."

The next hurdle I had to overcome was if she was going to pay in full or do payments. I asked her which one worked for her, and when she said, "I'll pay in full," I felt she could see my brain smiling through my forehead. I did play it cool, though, because I already envisioned this moment a thousand times in my mental rehearsals.

Orca Moment: Mental rehearsals are a future pacing technique to get your entire being used to living out the outcomes you want in life.

Overall this woman paid me $4,000 upfront for three months of work. I knew I could deliver because this is the level I knew I was supposed to be on. I felt that this was my time, and that this was my year to attract more clients like her. 2020, however, had different plans for all of us.

My 2020 plans were all about the next level of extreme growth. I wanted to be one of the best out in the coaching industry. I wanted people to know I had a great program that could really change their life forever. I wanted to make an impact in a way that people knew any and everything was possible for them to achieve—especially if they had someone like me in their corner holding space for them to be their best selves.

2020, however, was about to change everything. At the end of 2019, there were reports of a deadly virus out of Wuhan, China that doctors said had pneumonia-like symptoms and was killing people all over China. It was called coronavirus, also known as COVID-19.

In January and February here in America, we were just watching it and were still going on about life thinking it would just blow over. Most people in America—including the current president Donald Trump (or who people called 45)—downplayed the virus so much. It was as if it would never touch American soil, however everything was about to go to hell.

As the months went by, it was becoming more of a reality that COVID-19 was about to touchdown in America. Everyone was panicking. We were really facing something never seen before. The woman I was working with at the start of the year chose not to continue our coaching, and even my business relationship with Amanda went by the wayside.

Coronavirus started moving faster toward America, and it wouldn't stop anytime soon. We were living our everyday lives for the first three months of the year, until March 10 came around and we had to make a serious change in America.

March 10 was the day America had to go on timeout. All the plans everyone had for 2020 had just come to an abrupt end. We went into a phase of trying to figure out just what the hell we were all going to do with our lives. Thankfully, at this time I had my coach Jen and my mastermind group. Jen said, "Hey, we're going to attack this thing head-on like we're entrepreneurs. I'm going to coach you through it."

If it had not been for Jen Gaudet, I don't know what I would have done. A few months passed on and we started seeing things get worse and worse. The American economy was falling to shit. Stock prices were going down, hell, even the price of Bitcoin with it.

No one knew what to do. It was a very grim moment in our history, not just as a nation, but as human civilization as a whole. We were all locked down trying to work from home, trying to figure out how the hell we were going to move forward in this new life.

But not everything was down. Eventually, one thing started showing us a glimmer of hope. Something was finally showing why it was here once and for all. What gave us hope was Bitcoin. At last, it started to show its true power. Unlike the 2008 housing market crash, people now had a viable alternative to create wealth during what seemed to be similar to another great depression. This time, the world had another option to preserve wealth.

In March 2020 Bitcoin went low as $3,600, and then out of nowhere exploded to a price hovering around $8,000. During this time, I noticed just how unprepared I was for a real-life emergency, and I vowed to never repeat the situation. I started DoorDashing again. It was a helpful way to make money because you could really earn $100 in about two hours. The plus side was you didn't have to burn that much gas. Everyone was ordering food online and restaurants had to close their doors.

I remember telling Vonte all I was going to do was deliver DoorDash to buy necessities and buy bitcoin every day. That was one of the advantages of Bitcoin, you could buy whenever you chose to. While I was trying to figure things out, I remember reading a book by David Bach called *Smart Couples Finish Rich*. In it, he explains the power of compound interest and how investments can pay out over time with consistent effort of investing in your future self.

His book was referring to an investment that earned at least a ten percent return over the span of twenty years. He gave the example of how just five dollars could multiply tremendously. I knew I could cut that time down to almost one to five years depending on the amount of bitcoin I purchased. I knew bitcoin performed way better than any investment his book would recommend, however the principles of investing and saving little by little over an extended period of time is what I needed the most, and that's exactly the approach I took with DoorDash and Bitcoin at that time.

Even though 2020 and COVID-19 was a scary situation, part of me was prepared for this after reading a book called *The Future Is Faster Than You Think* written by Peter Diamandis and Steven Kotler. It was a book dedicated to the idea that new exponential technologies would soon converge together and move humans thousands of years into the future. I read this book when it first came out in January 2020, and it helped me realize that for these technologies to work, COVID-19 had to happen. It was a final farewell to the old ways of living. Reading that book was the one thing that helped shape my mind and prepare me to face a global pandemic. Reading, and always being willing to apply the knowledge I read, is what kept me sane during that time. All those years of hard work, and staying in a forward-thinking mindset, made this the opportune time to really dig into what I already knew about myself, which was to continuously move forward.

To prevail in life you have to continually be in the present while still making decisions that won't pay off until the future. If you have learned anything from this book, I hope you walk away with this: no matter what your current situation is, it was created by YOU, and you alone are responsible for changing it. You do that by constantly bettering yourself, constantly dreaming, building on that dream, and more importantly doing it in a way that will impact others.

The mindset of an orca or apex predator is to always rise above. These high-performing people know that even in their lowest moment, they will succeed as long as they stay the course and persevere through all situations.

I got a phone call from BitcoinZay. When I answered the phone he told me something profound.

"Justin, you remember the conversations we used to have four years ago about the world not being able to ignore Bitcoin anymore?"

"Yeah," I said.

"Well, that time is now," he said. "It's time for us to get to work, because the world is going to need us now more than ever."

That's when I knew I made the right decision investing in Bitcoin. This was going to be the thing that would save 2020 and the entire world.

As I end this book, I want you to never take your eyes off the ball. Never take your eyes off of what you innately feel is true, because when you feel it is the correct thing, time will always reward you. Time will always reward the people who stay committed to their craft. This book is all about being the orca, being the best and understanding what is needed to win. You might not see your own greatness now. Sometimes other people see greatness in us that we don't see in ourselves, however your job is to stay the course and continuously strive to be the best. Eventually, time will show you that you were great the entire time.

Made in the USA
Monee, IL
01 March 2022